BFI FILM CLASSICS
. . . .

Cinema is a fragile medium. Many of the great classic films of the past now exist, if at all, in damaged or incomplete prints. Concerned about the deterioration in the physical state of our film heritage, the National Film Archive, a Division of the British Film Institute, has compiled a list of 360 key films in the history of the cinema. The long-term goal of the Archive is to build a collection of perfect showprints of these films, which will then be screened regularly at the Museum of the Moving Image in London in a year-round repertory.

BFI Publishing has now commissioned a series of books to stand alongside these titles. Authors, including film critics and scholars, film-makers, novelists, historians and those distinguished in the arts, have been invited to write on a film of their choice, drawn from the Archive's list. Each volume will present the author's own insights into the chosen film, together with a brief production history and a detailed filmography, notes and bibliography. The numerous illustrations have been specially made from the Archive's own prints.

With new titles published each year, the BFI Film Classics series will rapidly grow into an authoritative and highly readable guide to the great films of world cinema.

Claire Trevor and John Wayne

BFI FILM CLASSICS

STAGECOACH

·····················

Edward Buscombe

BFI PUBLISHING

First published in 1992 by the
BRITISH FILM INSTITUTE
21 Stephen Street, London W1P 1PL

Copyright © Edward Buscombe 1992

Reprinted 1993, 1996

British Library Cataloguing in Publication Data

Buscombe, Edward
Stagecoach.
I. Title
791.4372

ISBN 0 85170 299 6

Designed by
Andrew Barron & Collis Clements Associates

Typesetting by
Fakenham Photosetting Limited, Norfolk
Printed in Great Britain by
The Trinity Press, Worcester

CONTENTS

ACKNOWLEDGMENTS

Even books as small as this have multiple parents. For help in its birth I need to thank Manuel Alvarado, Tino Balio, Sarah Boston, Roma Gibson, John Smoker, David Meeker and staff in the National Film Archive at the BFI, Harold L. Miller and the State Historical Society of Wisconsin, Colin Rattee and staff in the Stills, Posters and Designs Department at the BFI, Markku Salmi, David Sharpe and staff of BFI Library and Information Services, *et al*.

Thanks are due to the following for permission to reproduce pictures: Buffalo Bill Historical Center, Cody, Wyoming for the poster from Buffalo Bill's Wild West; University of Exeter Library for Edward S. Curtis, 'Canyon de Chelly, Navahos'; Wisconsin Center for Film and Theater Research for the pictures of John Ford at work; Museum of Western Art, Denver, Colorado for Frederic Remington, 'Downing the Nigh Leader'. Film stills are from the collection of the Stills, Posters and Designs Department of the British Film Institute.

'Hey, look, it's Ringo!'

I

....

It's one of the most stunning entrances in all of cinema. We hear a shot, and cut suddenly to Ringo standing by the trail, twirling his rifle. 'Hold it,' cries the unmistakable voice of John Wayne. The camera dollies quickly in towards a tight close-up – a rarity for Ford, whose preferred method of shooting was to plonk the camera down four-square and move the actors around it. So fast is the dolly in that the operator can't quite hold the focus. But as the camera settles securely on Wayne's sweat-stained face Buck, agog with the anticipation of excitement to come, calls out, 'Hey look, it's Ringo!'

Ringo is dressed in jeans, with the trouser bottoms rolled up and worn outside his boots. He wears army-style braces, a neckerchief and a placket-front shirt, which has a kind of panel buttoned on it. Wayne was to make this style of shirt his trademark, and Jane Gaines has suggested that it gives the wearer a kind of fortified or armoured look, reinforcing the authoritarian aura of the mature Wayne persona.[1] By 1938 there were two distinct styles of Western costume in the movies. One derived originally from the flamboyant outfits affected by such real-life Western self-publicists as George Armstrong Custer and Buffalo Bill Cody, who went in for elaborately fringed buckskin jackets, thigh-length boots and shoulder-length hair. Mingled with the influence of Mexican *vaqueros*, rodeo cowboys and the fantasies of showbiz, this style had been brought to a peak of extravagance in the 1920s by Tom Mix, whose sartorial flourishes were to be adopted wholesale by the singing cowboys of the later 1930s.

But there was another vital if less exuberant tradition, best exemplified in the early 1920s by William S. Hart. Though in some ways as stylised a performer as Mix, Hart claimed his films took a more realistic look at the old West. Characteristically his costume is more functional than fancy; it favours, in its use of gauntlets and heavy leather chaps, the protective rather than the ornamental.

Wayne, in *Stagecoach* and in all his subsequent Westerns, was squarely in the Hart tradition. But we are getting ahead of ourselves. His entrance is neither the beginning of *Stagecoach*, nor the start of Wayne's career. Though with the benefit of hindsight we are astonished by how young Wayne looks – fresh-faced almost – he was in fact already past thirty by this time. Born Marion Michael Morrison in Iowa in 1907, he had entered the University of Southern California on a football scholarship in 1926. While working as a prop man at the Fox studio during the vacation, he met John Ford and was given a bit part in Ford's *Hangman's House* (1928), his first credited role. The following year saw his first speaking part in Ford's *Men Without Women*. His big break came in 1930 when, now John Wayne, he was given the lead in Raoul Walsh's epic Western *The Big Trail*. Though the delivery of his lines is not always certain – few actors were confident in those very early days of sound – Wayne certainly looked the part. For those who know only the weather-beaten and rather portly figure of his later years, it might be hard to recognise the willowy and indeed beautiful young man he was then.

The Big Trail was not a box-office success, and though this was scarcely Wayne's fault he was condemned, on the principle that you are only as good as your last picture, to spend almost a decade on Poverty Row, eking out a living on a succession of cheap action pictures. For nearly ten years Wayne – or more often his double, Yakima Canutt – leaped aboard speeding trains, jumped out of aeroplanes and endured unspeakable privations in the French Foreign Legion. And he made Westerns, dozens of them, for Warners, Monogram and Republic. In some of them he even sang, dubbed in an implausible gravelly bass by Smith Bellew.

Of course what constitutes a living is relative. Wayne's rock-bottom point was his contract with Monogram, where he made $2,500 a picture and completed eight Westerns in 1933. You could live pretty well on $20,000 a year in the 1930s. But it wasn't the big time. Throughout the 1920s and 1930s there were (at least) two Hollywoods. There was the world of MGM, Paramount and the other major studios, each making fifty or so major features a year starring two or more of their galaxy of talent, the glittering cynosures of international renown such as Greta Garbo, Marlene Dietrich, Clark Gable or Ronald Colman. And then there was Poverty Row, the fly-by-night studios trying to squeeze a profit out of films produced at knock-down prices, for the specialised theatre circuits which catered for rural audiences in the South and West, or else shown as the lower half of a double bill. During the 30s the collapse at the box office caused by the Depression

John Wayne and Marguerite Churchill in *The Big Trail*

had led exhibitors to seek out any gimmick to lure patrons back. Bingo, popcorn, free gifts, all were tried. An enduring legacy was the double bill, in which audiences got two pictures for the price of one. A host of minor studios rushed to cash in on the opportunity this provided, supplying product for the lower, or 'B', half of the programme. Thus was born the B-Western, the dusty vineyard in which John Wayne laboured throughout his early manhood.

Wayne's career showed that it was possible to make the leap up from the lower depths into the sunlit pastures of stardom, but for the most part the two worlds kept themselves apart, two parallel industries supplying product for two polarised markets. Wayne's last film before *Stagecoach* was *Red River Range*, one of the 'Three Mesquiteers' series Republic had based on the novels of William Colt MacDonald. After he had finished working with Ford, Wayne went straight back to finish his contract with Republic, appearing in *The Night Riders* and three further films in the 'Three Mesquiteers' series. Republic held back the release of these until after *Stagecoach* appeared, hoping to take advantage of their leading man's advancement. They suspected, rightly, that this would be John Wayne's last appearance in series Westerns.

II

John Ford, by contrast, had been a top-notch film director for twenty years. His career had evolved through a number of distinct stages. He had begun in a milieu pretty much like that which Wayne inhabited during the 30s, the world of the series Western. Working as Jack Ford (he did not become 'John Ford' until *Cameo Kirby* in 1923), he had gained a little experience as an actor, mostly in pictures directed by his brother, Francis. In 1917 he became a director himself, and for the next ten years he made mostly action films, many of them Westerns starring Harry Carey, Hoot Gibson or Tom Mix. The summation of the early Ford Western was *The Iron Horse*, an epic story of the building of the transcontinental railroad which Ford directed for Fox in 1924.

After this Ford was to direct only one more Western, *Three Bad Men* in 1926, before embarking on *Stagecoach*. In the second half of the

20s and in the 30s, while keeping his hand in with action pictures like *Men Without Women* and *Airmail*, and an occasional comedy like *Riley the Cop*, Ford also became adept at melodramas such as *Arrowsmith*, made for Sam Goldwyn in 1931. Then in 1935 came another change of direction with *The Informer*, an arty and heavily atmospheric drama of Irish republicanism, based on the novel by Liam O'Flaherty. It won Ford numerous critical awards and a new reputation as a director of important films based on prestigious works of literature. In 1936 he followed with *Mary of Scotland*, taken from the play by Maxwell Anderson, and *The Plough and the Stars*, from Sean O'Casey's play. Even if his next picture, *Wee Willie Winkie* with Shirley Temple, was hardly classic material, Ford's reputation at the time he came to make *Stagecoach* had risen far above his lowly origins in the series Western.

A sure indication of his status at the end of the 1930s is the fact that Ford was being courted by David O. Selznick, one of the best-connected, most ambitious and respected producers in Hollywood, just a year or two away from his greatest triumph, *Gone With the Wind*. Selznick had not the remotest interest in the world of the series Western. What he saw in Ford was a director of quality pictures. Ford had first come into contact with Selznick through his involvement with Merian C. Cooper, the celebrated producer and co-director of *King Kong*. Cooper had formed a great admiration for Ford in the mid-30s while the latter was working at RKO, where Cooper had succeeded Selznick as vice-president in charge of production in 1933. Cooper had also formed a company named Pioneer with his friend John Hay ('Jock') Whitney, a wealthy New Yorker whose cousin, C.V. Whitney, would later produce Ford's masterpiece *The Searchers* with Cooper. In 1933 Pioneer had signed a contract with Technicolor to make eight feature films in the new three-colour Technicolor process.[2] Then, in 1936, Cooper threw in his lot with Selznick and merged Pioneer with Selznick International. An ambitious programme of pictures was announced, several of them in colour. Since Ford was already under contract to Pioneer, his contract was taken over by the new company.

Ford and Selznick could not get along. Two equally strong-willed but utterly different personalities, they rubbed each other up the wrong way from the beginning. Cooper's account of the abortive attempt by Selznick to secure Ford's services is instructive:

I thought Jack Ford was the very best director alive, so when Jock Whitney and I formed Pioneer, one of the first things I did was to make a deal with Ford to direct two pictures at $85,000 a picture. ... In the deal I made with David [Selznick] and Jock Whitney, I was to be vice-president of Selznick International. I was to pick my own pictures and have full authority for producing them, with David to have veto power of any picture I picked if he thought it would be a money loser, but with nothing to say once the picture was agreed to. Now about this time, Ford had read a short story in *Collier's* magazine called 'Stage to Lordsburg', which he bought the rights to and told me he wanted to make a picture of. ... Ford wanted John Wayne for the lead; I didn't know Wayne but I ran several pictures in which he appeared, *The Big Trail* and a couple of the 'Three Mesquiteers' pictures he'd done at Republic, and I agreed with Ford that he was perfect. I knew Claire Trevor, and Ford and I settled on her for the girl, and I told Ford to go ahead and verbally commit for both Wayne and Trevor, and then we went up to David Selznick's house for dinner to tell him about the picture, which we called *Stagecoach*.

To my surprise, David was not impressed. First he said we had no big name stars and secondly 'it was just another Western'. He said we'd do a lot better if we did a classic. ... Ford and I both jumped David hard on this. Jack Ford can state a case as well as anybody when he wants to take the time to do it; I'm not too bad myself, and over coffee, we argued that this was a *classic* Western with *classic* characters and we finally convinced him and got the go ahead. But the very next morning, David called and asked us to come in and see him and the very first thing he says was that he had given our 'Western' 'deep thought' and it was his studied conclusion that the picture would not 'get its print costs back' unless we put stars into the two leads. ... He thought we would be highly pleased when he told us that he could get Gary Cooper and Marlene Dietrich instead of Wayne and Trevor. I was dumbfounded. ... Besides the fact that they were bad casting, they were both too old, and I had given my word to both Wayne and Claire Trevor through Ford that we would use them. ... We argued all morning, but I couldn't shake him and he couldn't move me, so right then and there I resigned. ... After I left, Jack told David that he'd made a contract with me personally to make *Stagecoach* regardless of what company made the picture, so he left too.[3]

The terms of the disagreement between Selznick and the two friends are instructive. Selznick's dismissive description of the project as 'just another Western' places it firmly in that category of action film which Ford had cut his teeth on but which he had now risen above. Within the film industry the term 'Western' was by this time applied only to films of a lower order, with small budgets, mass-produced in series for a particular audience, largely male and mainly rural. Westerns were the kind of picture John Wayne had been making ever since the failure of *The Big Trail*, the kind he was desperate to get out of. In calling *Stagecoach* a Western, Ford didn't mean anything like that, and indeed when the film eventually appeared it was described in the trade press as a 'melodrama', not a Western at all.[4] Strictly speaking, within the industry the term 'classic Western' was an oxymoron. Ford's use of such a phrase signalled his intention to invent a new hybrid genre – or rather to reinvent it, in the way *The Covered Wagon* had done fifteen years before. He would distance himself from the B-feature by making a film which grafted some of the sturdy appeal of the traditional Western proper – chases, gunfights, spectacular scenery – on to the classier pedigree of the Hollywood A-feature of the late 1930s.

Virtually every decision Ford made in preparing his film was calculated towards that end. His casting, as we shall see, was a careful mix of Hollywood saddle tramps and respected character actors. As scriptwriter he chose a man already well-known for his skill in giving tone and class to popular genres, and in their work on the plot Ford and Dudley Nichols added elements, such as more love interest and the birth of the baby, which deliberately broadened the appeal of the story beyond the traditionally male spectators of Westerns. And so when the film was released the United Artists publicists were able to highlight in their promotional campaign numerous features, such as women's fashions, not usually associated with the Western.

Selznick, however, remained unimpressed. In a series of lengthy memos (not for nothing was he known as 'The Great Dictator'),

Selznick placed on record his irritation with Ford:

> We must select the story and sell it to John Ford, instead of
> having Ford select some uncommercial pet of his that we would
> be making only because of Ford's enthusiasm. ... I see no
> justification for making any story just because it is liked by a man
> who, I am willing to concede, is one of the greatest directors in
> the world, but whose record commercially is far from good. I saw
> *Wee Willie Winkie* the other night and it is anything but a great
> picture. ...[5]

Selznick displayed vexation and self-pity by turns:

> Ford has apparently no desire to go through with his
> commitment to us, evidently being annoyed because he could not
> do *The Stage to Lordsburg*. I don't think we should be chumps
> about this, and if Ford actually has a commitment with us I see no
> reason for releasing him. On the other hand, I have no particular
> desire to have him if he doesn't want to come here, and would be
> willing to trade him to some other studio for a director that we
> need. He is an excellent man, but there is no point in treating him
> like a god. ...
>
> I am somewhat wounded, since this is the first time in my
> career that anyone has said that he did not want to work for me,
> but I don't suppose there is anything I can do except bandage up
> the wound.[6]

III

Stagecoach must have seemed a pretty good prospect to make Merian C.
Cooper throw over all his plans with Selznick-International. But
Cooper now no longer had a guarantee of production finance, and
though out of friendship he continued to help Ford set up his picture,
Ford was forced to turn elsewhere for the money. According to Dan
Ford, the director's nephew and biographer, the project was touted all
round Hollywood. Darryl Zanuck at Fox refused even to read it.

Eventually it was picked up by Walter Wanger, at that time running his own company, Walter Wanger Productions, under the umbrella of United Artists. Wanger is described by Tino Balio in his history of United Artists as 'a gentleman of breeding, college educated, and given to making lofty pronouncements about the social responsibilities of the film-maker and his educational role in a democracy. . . . Wanger had the reputation for setting trends, for being daring yet tasteful, politically provocative yet having mass appeal.'

Ford was still setting his sights high, going for the top end of the market in producers. Wanger had something of a reputation as a star-maker, having 'discovered' Claudette Colbert, Maurice Chevalier and Ginger Rogers. Several major stars were under contract to him personally, including Charles Boyer, Henry Fonda and Joan Bennett. He had been in charge of prestige projects at Paramount, Columbia and MGM before coming to United Artists, who had offered him an attractive deal in the summer of 1936. United Artists would allow him complete control of all production matters and supply the financing with money borrowed from the Bank of America. This arrangement was facilitated by the fact that the chairman of the bank's general executive committee, which dealt with its film industry interests, was Dr Attilio H. Giannini, who had just been elected president and chairman of the board of United Artists.[7]

At first, things did not go well for Wanger at United Artists. In the two years up to 1938 the company put $2 million into seven Wanger pictures, but none had showed a profit. As UA saw it, Wanger had been overspending. The producer was therefore obliged to rein back his budgets. Ford's project to film 'Stage to Lordsburg' must therefore have appeared especially attractive to him: a talented, tested and prestigious director, relatively unknown and therefore inexpensive stars, and a type of story which, even if Westerns were not fashionable, was nevertheless of proven appeal. Ford was signed; shooting began on 31 October 1938 and lasted until 23 December.

There could no longer be any question of making the film in colour. Wanger's straitened circumstances at UA wouldn't run to the extra expense – in the mid-1930s colour added 30 per cent to production costs. The average cost of a feature film at that time was about $300,000, but this figure would cover many films made on very low budgets, as well as more expensive ones – a recent Wanger spectacular, *Walter Wanger's Vogues of 1938*, had cost $1.4 million.[8] The actual negative cost of *Stagecoach* was $531,374.13. This was slightly less than the planned budget, which totalled $546,200, broken down as follows:[9]

	$
Story	7,500
Continuity and Treatment	22,000
Players	87,000
Direction	50,000
Production Staff	23,600
Sets	50,300
Set Operation	26,900
Film	24,700
Wardrobe	7,000
Cutting	12,200
Location	15,600
Tests	1,000
Trucks & Auto Hire	16,900
Titles & Inserts	2,000
Music	15,000
Sound royalties	5,000
Insurance	9,400
Other Expense	26,100
Studio Rent	27,000
Studio Surcharge	7,000
General Overhead	110,000
TOTAL	546,200

So Ford was paid $50,000 to direct and Dudley Nichols $20,000 for his script (another $2,000 being spent on stenographers). The top-billing star, Claire Trevor, received only $15,000. (So much for the star system!) John Wayne, though billed as her co-star, could command no more than $3,700, scarcely more than his rate at Monogram. The other actors' fees were as follows:

	$
Andy Devine	10,624
Thomas Mitchell	12,000
George Bancroft	8,250
Donald Meek	5,416
Tim Holt	5,000
Louise Platt	8,541
John Carradine	3,666
Berton Churchill	4,500
Bits and extra talent	22,862

IV

. . . .

We have come now to look upon *Stagecoach* as a John Ford film, or perhaps a John Wayne film. But the first title on the screen announces 'Walter Wanger Presents', in a handwritten script. Wanger is thus the only person whose signature is literally on the film. The remainder of the titles follow in the familiar Playbill typeface, a style developed in the nineteenth century out of traditional woodblock printing, suitable for the large point sizes required for theatre posters and other public announcements. The special characteristic of this face is that the serifs are narrower than the main strokes. In the cinema Playbill is invariably associated with the Western, and Ford especially favoured it.

Wanger's name appears over a shot of a deserted Monument Valley. As further titles follow, the screen begins to fill with movement. In a series of shots a stagecoach, cavalry and Indians cross and recross the frame until the final title, 'Directed by John Ford', which appears over a stagecoach outlined against the sky, driving away from the camera.

The title in Playbill

V

. . . .

The film proper begins, as Westerns almost invariably do, with riders heading towards the camera. There's a cut to an army post as they ride in at speed, while a bugle sounds urgently. Inside the fort the two scouts report to a captain and a lieutenant. One word forms the burden of their exchange: Geronimo. Westerns often seek to anchor their stories in a legitimising historical reality by starting with a place and a date. Ford's later film *The Searchers* begins with the legend 'Texas, 1868'. *Stagecoach* has no such dateline, but the mention of Geronimo links the events of the film to a particular location and period, the Arizona border with Mexico during the period 1881–6, when Geronimo and his Chiricahua band of Apache had escaped the reservation and were playing cat and mouse with the US army.

We get some details of the Apaches' activities. They have burnt ranches (later we shall see evidence), and they have cut the telegraph wires, an action that has important consequences in the plot. For the

Chief Big Tree as the Cheyenne scout

film-maker the advantage of working in such a well-known genre is economy. So much can be assumed, so little needs explication. The name of Geronimo is itself enough to set the wheels of the narrative turning. The threat of attack is reinforced by a shot of the Indian scout. On the soundtrack we are reassured that he is friendly ('He's a Cheyenne. They hate Apaches worse than we do.'). But the close-up of his impassive face, lit from below to increase the menace, invites the audience to read into it all their worst fears.

The Indian is played by Chief Big Tree, a veteran whose screen career had begun in 1915. Ford used him a year later in *Drums Along the Mohawk*, where, again playing a friendly, he scares Claudette Colbert half to death. His last appearance for Ford is in *She Wore a Yellow Ribbon* (1949), where Chief Big Tree, by this time 84 years old, and John Wayne, a mere stripling of 42, agree they are too old for war.

Ford's casting of *Stagecoach* is virtually a résumé of Western film history. The white scout in the opening scene is played by Yakima Canutt, who had first appeared in a Western in 1919. As we shall see, Canutt had by 1938 established himself as not just an actor but the foremost Western stuntman in the business. The third player in this opening scene with a notable Western pedigree is Tim Holt, as young Lieutenant Blanchard. His father, Jack Holt, had been a major Western star in the 1920s, playing the lead in the Paramount trail driving epic *North of 36* in 1924. Tim was to go on to success as a B-Western star for RKO in the 1940s.

Ford was famously loyal to former employees. Ike, one of the Plummer brothers, is played by Vester Pegg. The sheriff of Lordsburg, a tiny part, is played by Duke Lee. Both actors had been regular fixtures in Ford's early silent Westerns. They each, for example, had an important role in *Hell Bent*, a Harry Carey Western which Ford directed in 1918 and which had long been thought lost until it turned up in the Czech film archive a couple of years ago. Two cowboys appear briefly in a later scene, played by Buddy Roosevelt and Bill Cody. Each had been a successful Western star in the 1920s, with his own series. By 1939 their careers as stars were over; *Stagecoach* allows them one last gleaming. Other actors with minor roles in the film whom Ford remembered from earlier days include Helen Gibson and Steve Clemente. A more substantial role is given to Tom Tyler, who had first appeared in Westerns in 1924 and who had spent much of the 1930s as Stony Brooke in the same 'Three Mesquiteers' series which Wayne had frequented.

Most intriguing of all in the line of descent which ties *Stagecoach* into the tradition of the Western and into Ford's own past is the casting of his brother Francis Ford in the part of Billy Pickett, the proprietor of the stagecoach station at Dry Fork. Fourteen years older than his brother, Francis was in the years before 1920 easily the more famous of the two; initially as an actor, then as the director of several hundred movies, many of them Westerns produced by Thomas Ince's 101 company. By the early 1920s, however, his career was in decline, and the roles he was assigned in his brother's films, dating from 1922, are minor, typically as amiable, drunken old-timers. In *Stagecoach* he doesn't speak a single word, communication between him and Doc Boone, his drinking companion, requiring no more than a wink and a leer. In Dudley Nichols' original script the part had several lines; John Ford as director cut them out. Tag Gallagher has suggested that John Ford was inordinately jealous of his older and initially more successful brother.[10] And it's possible that he deliberately gave his brother simpleton parts in order to humiliate him. But though Ford was undoubtedly capable of such petty acts, we might also recall that none in the Fordian universe is more blessed than the saintly fool.

VI

From the opening scene establishing the Indian threat which will spur the action, the film dissolves to the main street of Tonto and begins its work of introducing us to the group of stagecoach passengers who, all unknowing, are to cross paths with Geronimo. The screen is filled with a wonderful sense of anticipation, realised in the

The colt chasing the stagecoach up the main street of Tonto

movement and bustle of the little town. There is no director like Ford for finding the touch that gives a sense of real life caught on the screen. As the stage rattles by, a young colt canters free behind the older horses, swept along in the excitement.

In a series of deft interlocking scenes, the film performs the necessary exposition, each character no sooner presented than defined, placed in relation to the pattern of social and personal relationships which emerges. First in view is the stage driver, Buck Rickabaugh, played by Andy Devine, he of the bulky physique and incongruously squeaky voice. Buck's principal function is to be the comic coward, a kind of Falstaffian foil to the heroic Hal manifested in the Ringo Kid (real name Henry, we learn).

Next we are presented with Lucy Mallory (Louise Platt), seen through the window of the stationary stagecoach. Everything about her speaks gentility, as Buck acknowledges when he addresses her: 'You folks may as well stretch your legs ... your limbs, ma'am.' The euphemism serves to place the action of the film in the heyday of stuffy Victorian morality, the hypocrisy of which will become a major theme. Lucy, who is pregnant, has come out west to join her husband, a captain in the cavalry. Her gentility derives from her southern origins – the nearest thing in the United States to a landed aristocracy. Already a distinctive class structure is being sketched in.

VII
....

Keeping company with Lucy in the coach is a small ineffectual man named Peacock. His name will be a constant source of amusement, variously misremembered as Hancock and Haycock (the last, doubtless, an in-joke reference to Ernest Haycox, the author of the story on which the film is based). Peacock is a whiskey-drummer whose solemn manner and sober attire cause him, with typically Fordian humour, to be constantly mistaken for a preacher. (In the original script he explains that he had indeed intended to be a man of the cloth, but had inherited the whiskey business through his wife – a woman, we infer, not to be crossed.)

Another passenger, Hatfield, we first see as Lucy is about to enter the hotel. He arouses her curiosity because he appears to recognise her. She is told he is 'a notorious gambler'. His clothes fit the part: white hat, black topcoat, white vest with silk tie and jewelled stickpin, complete with cane and a little moustache and imperial. Gambling, a raffish dandyism and southern origins go hand in hand in the Western. Later we will discover that during the Civil War Hatfield served in a regiment commanded by Lucy's father. His own father is a judge and a member of the southern aristocracy. Out of shame for what he has become, Hatfield keeps this secret from Lucy until the moment of his death. He represents the fag-end of southern gentility, his personal fastidiousness, snobbery and exaggerated courtliness hardly serving to patch over the fact that he is not above shooting a man in the back. Several Ford films, like *Judge Priest* and *The Sun Shines Bright*, contain affectionate portraits of the Old South. And in 1902 Owen Wister's novel *The Virginian* had succeeded in transforming into literature a despised and second-rate literary genre, the Western tale, by the device of furnishing its hero with southern ancestry, thereby raising his social status. But in *Stagecoach* Ford's view of the south is notably unsentimental. Hatfield is the only one of the nine people who ride the stage to Lordsburg not to survive the trip. As Brian Henderson remarks, he has no place in the democratic West.[11]

VIII
....

Stagecoach has two main narrative strands. The first, established in the opening scene, is woven around the Indian threat to the travellers. This has a lengthy pedigree. The story of a journey through dangerous terrain forms the basis of *The Odyssey*, as well as mediaeval romances such as *The Faerie Queene*. That sense of the endless possibilities of adventure, always some new excitement along the trail, is surely one of the chief reasons for the Western's elemental and compelling narrative appeal. Its contemporary cinematic transformation, the road movie, appears to have plenty of mileage left.

In the course of the nineteenth century the raw material of history, the process of westward expansion into North America by European settlers, became transformed into a myth suitable for exploitation by the entertainment industry. One among many narrative episodes told and retold was that of the attack on a group of travellers in the wilderness by forces beyond the law, whether bandits or Indians. Of the possible variants (settlers in covered wagons, railroad trains), the stagecoach was already by the 1860s a popular choice. The first regular transcontinental stage line had been inaugurated by Butterfield's Overland Mail Company in 1858. Ben Holladay's Overland Stage Line, the company transporting the passengers in *Stagecoach*, dates from 1864 (though in fact it was amalgamated into Wells Fargo in 1866, well before the period in which the film's action is set). Attacks on stagecoaches were a popular motif in the lithographs, many drawn from famous paintings of the time, which were the chief source of pictorial decoration for homes and public places during the later part of the nineteenth century. The attack on the Deadwood Stage was a prominent part of the programme in Buffalo Bill's Wild West shows. It's not surprising, then, that in the early years of the cinema the Bison company, one of the first to specialise in the Western, had several stagecoaches among its stock in trade.[12]

The next character we meet is Curly Wilcox, marshal of Tonto, played by the bluff and burly George Bancroft. Everyone who boards the stage must have a reason for getting to Lordsburg. Curly's is simple: the Ringo Kid has busted out of jail intent on revenge against the Plummer gang, who have killed his father and brother. Buck reports that he has seen Luke Plummer in Lordsburg. Anticipating that Ringo will make his way there, Curly elects to ride shotgun on the stage to forestall the expected confrontation and recapture the Kid.

So now the second strand of the narrative has been laid out: a revenge plot. This is no less ancient in origin, the staple of much Renaissance drama and of the Victorian melodrama. It is driven by the hero's sense of personal honour, an inner compulsion rather than an external threat. In the Western, the revenge plot mobilises the code by which the hero lives. As laconically articulated by Ringo later in the film, this is lapidary in its brevity: 'There's some things a man just can't run away from.' The phrase is almost comic in its bravado, though more resonant than the equivalent in Haycox's story: 'A man can escape nothing.' The sentiment finds an echo in many another Western, as for example in Pernell Roberts' celebrated aphorism in Budd Boetticher's

BUFFALO BILL'
AND CONGR

ON THE STAGE C

WILD WEST
ROUGH RIDERS
OF THE WORLD ·

A. Hoen & Co.
BALTIMORE MD.

ACH · THE ORIGINAL DEADWOOD COACH,
MOST FAMOUS VEHICLE IN HISTORY.

Ride Lonesome: 'There's some things a man just can't ride around.'

Just what are these things, and why can't a man avoid them? Virtually all Westerns end with a climactic act of violence. This violence is necessary, inevitable, because the Western takes place on the frontier, where the rule of law which would protect the weak and innocent does not yet exist. Right can only be established through might. Because the conventions have been so long established, a film hardly needs to explain the nature of the threat, or the need to confront it. What it must do is establish beyond doubt the moral right of the hero to commit the act of violence which will ensure that good prevails over evil.

From this perspective the Western appears a very unchristian genre. The hero who wishes for respect must be prepared to offer violence in exchange for violence. The Old Testament ethic dominates. If the hero turns the other cheek there is no story. Perhaps it's not so odd that Westerns should be popular in the rural hinterland of America, the heart of the Bible Belt, since what is fundamentalism but a revision of the New Testament in favour of the Old?

But surely there is a law in Lordsburg? Isn't Curly there precisely to represent the forces of civilisation which have outlawed revenge, and is not Ringo's mission therefore illegitimate? The film goes to lengths to persuade us of the contrary. First, Ringo is established as transparently good. Second, the Plummers are unequivocally evil, and patently out of control. Third, civilisation, in the form it presents itself in Tonto, is at best a mixed blessing. Finally, Curly himself recognises that Ringo has not in fact had justice, and will not get it unless he takes the law into his own hands.

IX

. . . .

Immediately following Curly's decision to go to Lordsburg we cut to a scene at the Miners' and Cattlemen's Bank. Inside is Gatewood, the banker, receiving from the Wells Fargo agent a deposit of cash. Gatewood is played by Berton Churchill, a former New York union leader who had made a speciality of playing pompous, self-important minor officials and pillars of society. (He is the judge who sentences Paul Muni in *I Am a Fugitive from a Chain Gang*.) Ford had used him frequently: in *Dr Bull, Judge Priest, Steamboat 'Round the Bend* and *Four Men and a Prayer.* Churchill had also played an embezzling banker in 1934 in *Frontier Marshal,* the first film version of Stuart Lake's book about Wyatt Earp.

Gatewood is one of only two characters who have been added to the cast of the original story. He carries considerable ideological weight. As the money is handed over he delivers himself of a sententious axiom: 'What's good for the banks is good for the country.' (A pre-echo of the notorious statement delivered by industrialist Charles Wilson to a Congressional committee in 1952: 'What's good for General Motors is good for the country and what's good for the country is good for General Motors.') Bankers are rarely accorded much respect in the Western. They are viewed through the lens of a vague but persistent populism which originated in the nineteenth century and which held eastern capitalists responsible for the hardship which seemed the invariable lot of the small farmer in the western states.

Claire Trevor, Berton Churchill, Louise Platt

Gatewood is not only personally unpleasant – rude, selfish, pompous – but a crook who jumps aboard the stage with the bank's money, and thus a suitable scapegoat for the ire of the populists. Once en route he launches into a lengthy homily on government economic policy, in terms which engage not with issues of the time when the film is set but directly with the politics of the moment of the film's release. What Gatewood has to say is a tendentious comment upon the programme of Franklin D. Roosevelt's New Deal:

> I don't know what the government's coming to. Instead of protecting businessmen it pokes its nose into business. Why, they're even talking now about having bank examiners. As if we bankers don't know how to run our own banks. Why, Boone, I actually have a letter from a popinjay official saying that they were going to inspect my books. I have a slogan which should be blazoned on every newspaper in the country. America for Americans. The government must not interfere with business. Reduce taxes. Our national debt is something shocking. Over one billion dollars a year. What this country needs is a businessman for President.

This was a highly charged statement for any film to make in 1939. Roosevelt had by then twice been elected on a platform of which the rhetoric and to some considerable extent the substance had been directed against big business, which was popularly held responsible for the economic disaster which had hit the country. Directly challenging the laissez-faire policies of the Republicans, FDR had launched a crusade against the right of business to mismanage its own affairs while the country went to pieces. The banks had been singled out for special opprobrium. Back in 1932 a major investigation into Wall Street led by Senator Pecora had uncovered widespread fraud and chicanery; banks had speculated in their own stock, advised investment clients to buy securities in companies which were in fact their own affiliates, and engaged in a host of other unscrupulous practices. Public anger was expressed by another senator, Wheeler of Montana (significantly, a western state), who exclaimed: 'The best way to restore confidence in the banks would be to take these crooked presidents out of the banks and treat them the same as we treated Al Capone when he failed to pay his income tax.'[13]

Two New Deal measures, the Banking Acts of 1933 and 1935, had greatly increased the powers of the central regulatory authority, the Federal Reserve Board. The reaction of the financial establishment had been to brand Roosevelt as little better than a Communist. Gatewood's outburst at 'interference' would undoubtedly have been read by audiences of 1939 as an echo of these protests. One of the very few bankers who supported Roosevelt's reforms was the very Dr Giannini who was president of United Artists at the time *Stagecoach* was being made, and who was popularly supposed to be the model for Dickson, the kindly and progressive banker in Frank Capra's 1932 film *American Madness*.

Gatewood's attempt to link his 'hands off the banks' plea to a xenophobic slogan of 'America for Americans' is, in the context of the Fordian universe, further evidence of his delinquency. Ford, himself fiercely proud of his Irish origins, peopled film after film with a rich diversity of national and ethnic types. The reactionary politics noisily espoused by John Wayne in the 1960s and 70s have much to do with the contemporary conception of the Western as ineluctably a WASP affair, incurably sexist, capitalist and racist. Yet historically, it is at least as plausible to see Westerns as fundamentally anti-establishment, against the rich and powerful and in favour of the poor and weak. Besides the triumphalism of conquest and empire-building, there is another tradition in the Western, the tradition that in the legend of Jesse James supports poor share-croppers against the banks and railroads, in the myth of Billy the Kid sides with honest ranchers against the corruption of the 'Santa Fe Ring', and in the saga of Joaquin Murieta enlists in the cause of persecuted Mexicans against their Anglo oppressors. The Western teems with corrupt sheriffs, arrogant and tyrannical landowners, grasping and cheating bankers, sadistic and blinkered martinets. Even on the racial issue, where the depiction of Indians makes it vulnerable, one might venture that there is more explicit anti-racism in the Western between 1940 and 1970 than in any other Hollywood genre. Only to the charge of sexism is one bound to enter a plea of guilty as charged.

Ford's own politics have confused his critics. In later life his close friendship with right-wingers such as Wayne and Ward Bond, and his close identification with the US military, seemed to indicate a move away from his earlier radicalism. In the 1930s he certainly thought of himself as a man of the left. In 1937 he wrote to his nephew Bob Ford: 'Politically, I am a definite socialist democrat – always left.' A Catholic, he had contributed $1,000 towards an ambulance for the Loyalists in the Spanish Civil War, though the Catholic establishment in the United States supported Franco.[14] The year after *Stagecoach* Ford would film Steinbeck's radical Depression epic *The Grapes of Wrath*, a film which has several interesting parallels with *Stagecoach*. Both tell the story of a journey through danger, hopefully towards a place of safety. In each bankers are villains, and the dispossessed are the heroes. The central figure in both films is a social outcast, the object of secret admiration for having, at least supposedly, 'busted out' of jail.

X

....

Gatewood's politics are utterly discredited by his personal iniquity. His windy rhetoric is also tellingly undercut by the character to whom it is ostensibly addressed. While Gatewood speaks, Doc Boone is rifling methodically through the samples case of the feebly protesting Peacock in search of another drink. To Gatewood's final exhortation, 'What this country needs is a businessman for President,' Doc's deflating response is 'What this country needs is more fuddle.' In a telling exchange with Jerry, the bartender in Tonto, Doc has already distanced himself from Gatewood's business philosophy. He prefaces his request for one last drink on the slate by admitting to Jerry, 'as one man to another ... economically I haven't been of much value to you.' As always in Ford, economic value and human value are not related. The drink is freely given, though there is no profit in it.

We first see Doc Boone in Tonto, being evicted by his harridan of a landlady, a woman with a pronounced English accent – the English rarely come well out of Ford's films. He is in the honourable tradition of drunks in Ford Westerns. Most drinking in Ford is comic. There are bravura performances by Victor McLaglen in *She Wore a Yellow Ribbon* and by Edmond O'Brien in *The Man Who Shot Liberty Valance*, which for good measure also has a drunken doctor in a minor role. In *My Darling Clementine* Victor Mature is the alcoholic Doc Holliday, though the role is not played for laughs. Thomas Mitchell had already practised for his *Stagecoach* role by playing a drunken doctor in *The Hurricane* in 1937, and followed up with a drunken newspaperman in *Mr Smith Goes to Washington* in 1939.

Quite why the stereotype of the drunken doctor should be so persistent in the Western (and not only in Ford's films) is hard to say. Why not drunken undertakers, or barbers, or schoolteachers or sheriffs? Perhaps the fall from grace is more pitiable in a professional man – and more reprehensible. Out on the frontier the doctor is the one specialist who cannot be replaced; if he becomes incapable no one else can take over. But there is also for Ford an association between drinking and having an education, as if the mere fact of being educated in the West is productive of an alienation which can only be anaesthetised by drink. Dutton Peabody, the editor in *Liberty Valance*, is a literate and articulate man – and a complete soak. In *My Darling Clementine* Doc Holliday quotes Shakespeare while drinking himself to death. And as Doc Boone is put on to the street by his landlady he addresses her with a couple of (mis)quoted lines from Marlowe's *Dr Faustus*: 'Is this the face that wrecked a thousand ships/And burnt the towerless tops of Ilium?' Doc knows history as well as literature. Giving his arm to Dallas, the prostitute who is another victim of the 'foul disease called social prejudice', he ironically invokes the French Revolution: 'Take my arm, Madame la Comtesse. The tumbril awaits. To the guillotine!' In the original version of the script which Dudley Nichols wrote from Ernest Haycox's story, Doc Boone elaborates this to: 'Driver, the Place de Grève.'

XI
....

In the late 1930s Nichols was known as a specialist in writing scripts based on prestigious literary originals. He had become a regular scriptwriter for Ford, working on *The Informer*, *Mary of Scotland* and *The Plough and the Stars*. Later he would write *The Long Voyage Home*, based on a Eugene O'Neill play, and *The Fugitive* from Graham Greene's *The*

Power and the Glory. Nichols has been burdened with a reputation for adaptations which were talky and showed an excessive reverence for the original text. 'The Ford-Nichols movies,' Tag Gallagher remarks, 'were characterised by literary pretence, theatrical value, and heavy Germanic stylisation.'[15] On this basis Nichols would seem an odd choice to write Ford's first Western for a dozen years.

Gallagher's description is at fault. Nichols could turn his hand to all kinds of films. He wrote several of Ford's successful action pictures of the 30s, and had a knack for the formula in which a small group is placed in jeopardy, as in two Ford vehicles *Men Without Women* and *The Lost Patrol*. The year before *Stagecoach* he had scripted *Bringing Up Baby*, the classic screwball comedy with Cary Grant and Katharine Hepburn, and *Carefree*, the hit musical with Astaire and Rogers. Later in his career Nichols moved quite away from the literary material he had occasionally favoured earlier. Six of his last eight pictures were Westerns. Looking at his work both for Ford and for other directors, one is inclined to conclude that though he may have sometimes been drawn to the artistically pretentious, his real forte was not in adapting intellectual work into a more popular medium, but rather the reverse, taking what was essentially pulp fiction and giving it a bit of class.

Certainly the picture which Ford made as *Stagecoach* is substantially the one in Nichols' script. True, some characteristic Ford touches are added. The scene at the end where Luke Plummer staggers into the saloon, apparently the victor in the shoot-out, only to drop dead on the floor, is Ford's addition, melodramatic but undeniably effective. And the very last dialogue exchange has been added to the script, as Curly lets Ringo and Dallas go and Doc remarks, 'Well, they're saved from the blessings of civilisation.' But even some things which seem quintessentially Ford were written by Nichols. The pan preceding the Indian attack, across Monument Valley, from the stage below up to Geronimo and his band poised on a clifftop, is specified by Nichols:

> The road winds through the canyon and the stagecoach comes into view and rolls slowly towards the mouth of the canyon. Then the view moves up and around to the rim of the canyon wall, and we see a band of savage-looking Apaches, their

foreheads smeared with white warpaint, lurking in ambush, waiting for the stagecoach to enter the canyon below. At their center stands the most dreaded figure in the Southwest, Geronimo, powerful of frame, with a craggy face that seems carved out of red rock.

Ernest Haycox's 'Stage to Lordsburg' was published in *Collier's* magazine on 10 April 1937, with a full-colour illustration of a mounted Apache above the title. Ford bought the movie rights, for a mere $2,500 he told *Action* magazine in 1971, though, as we have seen, the budget records $7,500. Haycox was a successful writer who specialised in Westerns. Much of his work appeared in pulp magazines such as *West*, but he also published in the more up-market 'slicks' (named for their better quality paper), magazines such as *Collier's*, and *The Saturday Evening Post*. His novel *Trouble Shooter* formed the basis for Cecil B. DeMille's *Union Pacific*, also released in 1939.

In selecting a story out of *Collier's*, Ford was choosing material a cut above the kind which formed the usual basis for B-Westerns. But in 'Stage to Lordsburg' Haycox had provided no more than the bare bones of a plot and some lightly sketched characters. Nichols' script expands and enriches the story. Several characters remain in essence the same; the original contains equivalents of Lucy, Peacock, Hatfield, Dallas, Ringo, Curly and Buck. Haycox also included a cattleman and an Englishman carrying 'an enormous sporting rifle'. Since neither is given much to do in the story, nothing is lost when they are excised from the screenplay. In their place we have Doc Boone and Gatewood.

All the names are changed. Buck was originally Happy Stuart, and Curly was John Strang. The originals of Peacock, Hatfield and Lucy have no names. Dallas had been named Henriette, and Ringo was Malpais Bill. The effect of these alterations is not radical, but they lend the film a more familiar Western feel. Buck, in the Western context, is an abbreviation for buckaroo, itself a bastard form of *vaquero*, the Spanish word for a cowboy. Doc Boone is an obvious echo of Daniel Boone, the Pathfinder. Dallas, after the city in Texas, has a more authentic south-western sound than Henriette. The Western antecedents of Ringo date back at least as far as Johnny Ringo, who had a gunfight with Doc Holliday in Tombstone in 1882. Holliday was a close friend of Wyatt Earp and Ford had come to know Earp in Hollywood in the late 1920s. Stuart Lake's fanciful biography of the lawman, *Wyatt Earp, Frontier Marshal*, became the basis of Ford's film *My Darling Clementine*. Rudy Behlmer suggests that some of the names in Lake's book may have been borrowed by Nichols, Wes Wilcox becoming Curly Wilcox, Lou Rickabaugh changing to Buck Rickabaugh and Jim Peacock transformed into Samuel Peacock.[16] Other names reverberate with the history of the West and its later manifestations in show business. The brothers from whom Ringo seeks revenge are named Plummer. Henry Plummer was sheriff of Bannack, Montana, in the 1860s, where he led a murderous gang of bandits and was eventually hanged by vigilantes. The proprietor of the stage station at Dry Fork, Billy Pickett, shares his name with a famous black rodeo star who appeared in a number of 'race' movies in the 1920s.[17]

Other significant differences from Nichols' script are that Malpais Bill is not an escaped prisoner, but boards the stage in Tonto like everyone else, and no baby is born en route. Haycox's whiskey salesman is a more disreputable character, who eventually succumbs not to an Apache arrow but to the heat. Henriette displays her Christian charity not by caring for a baby but by succouring the salesman before he dies. One effect of Nichols' changes is to deepen the divisions between polite society and the social outcasts, most especially by putting Malpais Bill on the same side as Dallas, moving the whiskey drummer up the social ladder and adding one character to each side in the persons of Doc Boone and Gatewood.

Ford remarked to Peter Bogdanovich: 'It was really "Boule de suif", and I imagine the writer, Ernie Haycox, got the idea from there ... '[18] Commentators have generally poured cold water on the notion that the story owes a serious debt to Maupassant's tale of a stage ride through enemy lines in Normandy during the Franco-Prussian war of 1870, and certainly there are major differences. Except for the character of the prostitute Boule de suif herself (literally, 'bowl of suet', so called because she has a ripely rounded figure), none of the characters corresponds closely to those in 'Stage to Lordsburg'.

What Maupassant's story and Nichols' script do have in common is an acute class consciousness. Maupassant is scornful of the hypocrisy of the prosperous bourgeoisie and the snobbery of the fading aristocrats, who combine to bully Boule de suif into securing their free passage through enemy lines by sleeping with a Prussian officer. Only too friendly while she has the key to their fate, they treat her with cold disdain once she has performed the act that secures their release. It's some indication of the Pecksniffian prudery of the Hollywood Production Code that a story written in 1880 is far more forthright in its description of Boule de suif's profession and her manner of conducting it than a movie made sixty years later. But the themes are strikingly similar. Nichols' script is similarly sharp in its depiction of the pretensions, cruelties and petty vanities of the pillars of society, as against the human charity displayed by the outcasts they despise: the whore, the drunk and the outlaw. Virtually every exchange between the major characters in the film works to deepen our appreciation that respectability and morality are very far from being the same thing.

XII
....

Doc and Dallas are introduced together. As she is being ejected from the town of Tonto by the ladies of the Law and Order League – respectability in action – so he is being shown the door by his landlady, herself a member of the League. Dallas and Doc are, as he proudly and appositely acknowledges, the 'dregs' of the town.

Dallas is never actually named as a prostitute, but only the young and innocent Ringo does not instantly recognise her profession. She is that familiar type beloved of melodrama, the soiled dove of the Victorian stage. The 'tart with a heart' entered the Western through Bret Harte's stories of the California mining camps. Ford himself had filmed Hart's 'The Outcasts of Poker Flat' in 1919, though the film has since been lost. One character in the story is a prostitute known as the Duchess. The central figure is John Oakhurst, the prototype of the elegant gamblers who wander through the Western, of whom Hatfield is a variation.

Claire Trevor is perfectly cast against John Wayne. Marlene Dietrich would have exoticised the character, giving her more glamour than the role could bear. Claire Trevor has a harder, more brassy look. She had been in films since the early 1930s, playing an assortment of molls and floozies. At the time of shooting she was only 29 to Wayne's 31, but she looks older than he. Appropriately enough; she understands, as he does not, that this is her last chance at happiness.

XIII

The scene is now set. Once Ringo has climbed aboard, the stage has its full complement of nine characters, seven passengers inside and Buck and Curly on top. Each character is defined both through his or her social position, a place in the general scheme of things, and in terms of an individual personality. Social position is plotted unambiguously, on either side of the line that separates the respectable from the rest. Lucy, Gatewood, Hatfield and Peacock are identified as belonging to polite society by their dress and general demeanour, but even more so by the fact that each recognises the other as belonging. So too the 'dregs' instinctively band together. Buck and Curly occupy a third space, neither bourgeois nor bohemian: the honest sons of toil.

Personal qualities too are for the most part plainly positive or negative. Gatewood is a bullying hypocrite, Ringo a brave and upright hero. The puny Peacock is comically cowardly but good-hearted, as is, in his different social station, the portly Buck. Lucy and Hatfield are cold and disdainful, until each in their way redeems their arrogance. Doc and Dallas are dissolute, but their hearts are warm and their vices are forgiven, since for Ford the real sins are those of omission, not commission.

XIV

The stage leaves town, accompanied by a troop of soldiers who will escort it as far as Dry Fork. From a wide shot of the stage trundling along through the landscape we cut to a two-shot of Buck and Curly on top. Curly is mystified how Gatewood could, as he has claimed, have received a telegram requiring his urgent presence in Lordsburg when, as we have already seen, the Indians have cut the wires. Buck, oblivious, muses on his domestic problems. We cut to inside the stage, where Gatewood first learns about the Apache threat. There is another cut to a long-shot of the stage and back to the two-shot of Buck and Curly, still talking at cross purposes. Then follow two more shots of the stage moving through the landscape before we meet Ringo.

This pattern is repeated throughout the film, scenes inside the stage or on top punctuated by bridging shots of the terrain through which it travels. These bridging shots perform a dual function. First, they indicate the passage of time, serving to facilitate the telescoping of the two days of the narrative into the ninety-minute duration of the film. Second, the repeated shots of landscape anchor the film securely in a locale, give it an authentic feel of a highly specific outside; make it, in fact, a Western.

Stagecoach was the first film John Ford made in Monument Valley, though he was not the first to discover its cinematic possibilities. *The Vanishing American*, based on the Zane Grey novel and made in 1925, has some opening sequences which are recognisably in this location. And in the years since Ford's films made Monument Valley the most

John Ford (left) on location with Tim Holt

recognisable icon in the Western landscape, others have exploited its visual impact. It forms the backdrop to the opening number sung by Judy Garland in the Western musical *The Harvey Girls* (1945). It appears, memorably, in Sergio Leone's *Once Upon a Time in the West* (1968). Lately, its imaginative currency risks being devalued by repeated use in television advertising, most recently in a Burger King commercial in which two fliers land a plane in the valley to pick up some fast food.

There are at least three different stories of how Ford came upon the site. To Peter Bogdanovich, Ford stated baldly: 'I knew about it. I had travelled up there once, driving through Arizona on my way to Santa Fe, New Mexico.'[19] In Maurice Zolotow's biography of John Wayne, the star claims that he introduced Ford to the valley, which he had himself first found in 1929.[20] A more intriguing account was published in 1978, when Todd McCarthy tracked down Harry Goulding, who with his wife had arrived in the valley in 1920 as the original white settlers and who ran Goulding's Trading Post and Lodge. Goulding's story is that in 1938 he was so distressed by the poverty of the Navaho living in the valley that he decided to go to Hollywood to try to interest a movie company in making a film there. Through sheer persistence he managed to get in to see Ford, at that time in discussion with Walter Wanger about *Stagecoach*. Goulding succeeded in talking Ford into flying up to take a look, and the rest is history. Or myth.[21]

Monument Valley stretches some thirty miles, straddling the border between Utah and Arizona. Its characteristic tower-like mesas of DeChelly sandstone, a thousand feet high, have been hewn from the desert floor by the action of wind and water over millions of years. Though its silhouettes have now become so familiar as to approach cliché, few tourists visit the site, which is in a remote part of the empty great south-west, on the way to nowhere in particular. In the 1930s, when such a thing mattered, it was the furthest place in the continental United States from a railroad – 180 miles.

Ford came to know the valley well. Besides *Stagecoach*, he shot six other films there: *My Darling Clementine, Fort Apache, She Wore a Yellow Ribbon, The Searchers, Sergeant Rutledge* and *Cheyenne Autumn*. Monument Valley forms part of the reservation of the Navaho, the largest group of

Native Americans, today numbering over 160,000 people. Ford got to know the Navaho, and used them in his films to play Apaches, Comanches, Cheyenne or whatever the story required. According to Tag Gallagher, he paid them union rates and was adopted into the tribe, being given the name of 'Natani Nez' – 'Tall Soldier'.[22] A spot on the 17–mile unpaved road you take to tour the valley is called 'John Ford's Point'.

Many of the cultural meanings we now invest in landscapes are of comparatively recent origin. Prior to the late eighteenth century, the aesthetic sensibility was not pleasurably stimulated by vast panoramas, towering cliffs, limitless vistas. The absence of human habitation was regarded with distaste. Hence the revolutionary effect of the Lakeland poets. Our modern taste for the west as a landscape of awesome grandeur, unspoilt by the marks of progress and civilisation, originated in the 1860s and 1870s with a small group of intrepid artists who journeyed west in search of a vision of the sublime. This they had imbibed under the influence of European Romanticism, especially the school of German Romantic painting based in Düsseldorf, where several of them, including the influential Albert Bierstadt, had studied. Photography was also coming into its own at that time, and had a considerable effect on the painters. Beginning in the 1860s, the photographer Carleton Watkins made a series of studies of Yosemite which so aroused the public enthusiasm for wilderness landscapes that Yosemite soon became the first area within the United States to be officially preserved for the people by Congress. Also in the 1860s Timothy O'Sullivan accompanied the geologist Clarence King on his expeditions into the 'Great American Desert', returning with a set of images which were ahead of their time in their appreciation of the beauty of canyons and mesas. Around the turn of the century, Edward S. Curtis produced a remarkable set of landscapes which anticipate the Western film's love of space and distance. What Ford found in Monument Valley, then, was a location which he could map on to a collective imagination nourished with the images of earlier artists.

Two hundred and fifty years ago Monument Valley would have appeared to the visitor as, in the parlance of the time, horrid; today the sight of it will conjure profound emotions in the most blasé tourist. On a shelf in my study I have a small piece of rock I brought home as a

souvenir. Notices placed by the Navaho guardians of the site say that the taking of samples is forbidden, but I had come six thousand miles and I couldn't resist. I think – I hope – the notice is to deter people hacking pieces off the cliffs. My little stone was already lying on the ground. It's deep brick-red in colour, quite soft to the touch. If you rub it hard a fine dust comes off on your finger – hence the comparative ease with which wind and rain have eroded the rocks. But it's not the colour or the texture which impresses in *Stagecoach*; Ford's first colour film in the valley, *She Wore a Yellow Ribbon*, came ten years later. What really counts is the sheer size and distance. In the clear, high atmosphere you can easily see for thirty or forty miles. (Monument Valley is 5,000 feet above sea level, which means it can get cold – hence the snow in *Stagecoach*.) In the vast panoramas across which Ford pans his camera, the tiny ark of the stagecoach appears pitifully frail.

It isn't just space that gives the valley its special aura; it's time. Victorian painters and photographers were profoundly influenced by geology. Since the publication of Charles Lyell's *Principles of Geology* in

Driving through Monument Valley in the snow

the early 1830s, which laid the foundations of our modern understanding of geological time, no one can look at such a spectacularly eroded landscape without reflecting on the eons which separate us from the creation of the earth. The layered tiers of the great sandstone towers are eloquent testimony to the countless millennia which have been etched upon their surfaces. Inescapably we are brought face to face with the brevity of human life as measured against the age of the earth. The human dramas which Ford plays out against this backdrop gain in poignancy from our sense of their tenuous grip upon such an ancient terrain.

Though a real place, Monument Valley functions in *Stagecoach* as imaginary geography. The journey supposedly takes two days. The passengers leave Tonto in the morning (before noon, since Gatewood's wife tells him dinner will be at twelve o'clock). They spend the night at Apache Wells, and arrive in Lordsburg after dark the next day. When they leave Tonto at the outset of the journey they enter Monument Valley. Yet when Ringo and Dallas drive out of Lordsburg together in

the final shot, they are still recognisably in Monument Valley. Sometimes virtually the same shot is used at widely separated parts of the narrative. As the stage comes up to Dry Fork for its first stop, there is a long slow pan across a huge expanse of the valley floor, with the stage a tiny spot in the distance, framed by the huge pinnacles of, from right to left, Merrick Butte, East Mitten and West Mitten. (The shot is taken from the approximate position of the present-day Visitors' Center.) An almost identical shot appears much later – by which time the stage should be miles further on – showing the stagecoach on the

Above left and right: Two separate scenes in Monument Valley

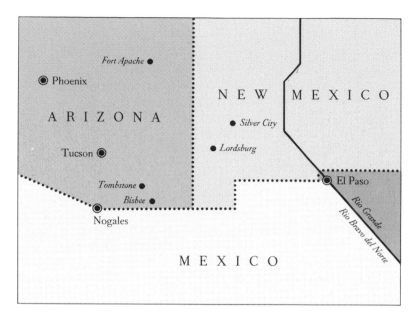

valley floor and then panning across to reveal Geronimo and his warriors waiting on a promontory. This contrast of apparent progression yet actual stasis is odd in a genre so predicated on movement as the Western. Ford's fondness for Monument Valley produced even more marked effects of circular motion in *The Searchers*, where Ethan and Marty journey for seven years, hardly ever leaving the Monument Valley location; and in *Cheyenne Autumn*, where the thousand-mile journey of the Cheyenne never takes them beyond its borders.

Another curious aspect of the film's geography is the actual direction the journey is supposed to take. One naturally supposes, given that the stagecoach is leaving an area of settlement and striking out across hostile, Indian-occupied territory, that its progress is westward. But this is not in fact the case. At the beginning we are told the stage has come to Tonto from Bisbee. Its final destination is Lordsburg. Bisbee is situated in the south-eastern corner of Arizona. As the map shows, to get to Lordsburg, in New Mexico, you must travel north-east.

XV

....

Once Ringo has climbed aboard, the party is complete. On top, Buck drives and Curly rides shotgun. Inside the stage the passengers have also formed into couples: Dallas and Ringo, the romantic leads; Lucy and her self-appointed guardian, Hatfield; Doc Boone and his whiskey-supplier, Peacock. Gatewood is a pariah.

The stage sets off, seen in a wide shot as it rolls through Monument Valley. We hear again the jaunty theme which was first played as the stage rattled into Tonto, and which is repeated every time we have an exterior shot along the trail. The musical score for the film is a tissue of familiar tunes, most of them traditional. According to some sources there are seventeen in all. The pressbook for the film lists the following: 'Gentle Annie', 'Jeanie With the Light Brown Hair', 'Shall We Gather at the River', 'Ten Thousand Cattle', 'She's More To Be Pitied Than Censored', 'She May Have Seen Better Days', 'Lilly Dale', 'Rosa Lee', 'My Lulu', 'Joe Bowers', 'Joe the Wrangler', 'The Trail to Mexico' and 'Careless Love'.

'Shall We Gather at the River', often played at moments of intense emotion in Ford films, is for once used ironically, as a kind of comic funeral march in the scene when Dallas is being drummed out of Tonto by the Ladies Law and Order League. 'Jeanie With the Light Brown Hair', the Stephen Foster standard, is the theme music for Lucy Mallory. Strangely, though one would suppose Dallas to be the romantic lead in the film (Claire Trevor receives top billing), she has no real theme tune of her own, only some rather tuneless chords played during her emotional moments with Ringo. The romance is low-key. They do not get to kiss once in the film, being restricted to a rather desperate hug at the end after Ringo has killed the Plummers. It may be that self-censorship in response to the Production Code's strictures against 'immorality' (Dallas is after all a prostitute) prevented the love story being given the full Hollywood treatment.

Most of the tunes listed in the pressbook are packed into a piano medley which plays virtually throughout the final sequence in Lordsburg, the music being motivated at one moment by a cut to a piano player in the saloon where Luke Plummer is playing cards. Apart from this sequence, and the Spanish song sung by Chris's Indian wife, of which more later, the only other music of any substance in the film is the stagecoach theme itself. Rudy Behlmer says that this theme is 'Bury Me Not on the Lone Prairie', a cowboy folk song first printed in the celebrated collection of John Lomax, published as *Cowboy Songs and Other Frontier Ballads* in 1910. This seems hard to believe. The pressbook doesn't mention it, and though there are some similarities in the tune, 'Bury Me Not' is a very lugubrious song, sung in a slow tempo in keeping with its sentiments:

> Oh bury me not on the lone prairie,
> These words came low and mournfully
> From the pallid lips of a youth who lay
> On his dying bed at the close of day.

The stagecoach theme sounds more like a much jollier ballad, 'The Trail to Mexico', which the pressbook does mention. This, say the instructions on Lomax's version, is to be sung with 'vigor and intensity':

However, Behlmer has seen the music sheets at Paramount

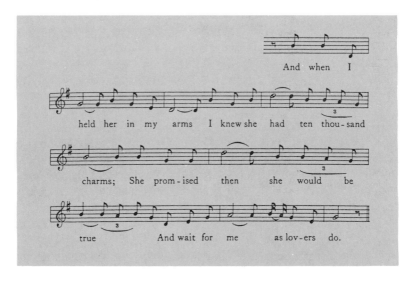

A few bars from 'The Trail to Mexico'

Studios, to whom the score was farmed out, so presumably he has some evidence for his attribution.[23] Louis Gruenberg was to have done the score, but for some reason this did not work out. The music sheets list John Leipold, Leo Shuken, Gerard Carbonara, W. Franke Harling and Richard Hageman as all contributing; several composers were needed because of the film's speedy release schedule. Carbonara's name does not appear on the screen, but Gruenberg's does even though his music was not used. The 1939 Oscar for best score went to all except these last two. Hageman's skill at weaving folk songs into a finished score was clearly a hit with Ford, who used him on six other films: *The Long Voyage Home*, *The Fugitive*, *Fort Apache*, *3 Godfathers*, *She Wore a Yellow Ribbon* and *Wagon Master*.

XVI

Inside the stage, alliances are being formed and feuds developed. Doc establishes that he once treated Ringo's brother for a broken arm; he firmly resists an invitation by Hatfield to refer to 'the War for the Southern Confederacy' instead of 'the War of the Rebellion'. Hatfield, asserting his Southern gallantry, retaliates by demanding Doc puts out his cigar, which is bothering 'the lady'. Doc counters that Hatfield, despite his pretensions to being a gentleman, is a back-shooter. Ringo, pre-announced as the man of violence, enforces peace by sheer force of character. Before things can develop further the stage arrives at Dry Fork.

The wife of Billy Pickett, the way-station manager, has a broad Scottish accent, unusual in Ford's west, where the Irish easily outnumber other Celts. She greets the passengers warmly but with surprise. She has heard about the Apache and supposed that no stage would run. When it becomes clear that there are no soldiers to escort them on further, the passengers face a dilemma: to return with the soldiers who have brought them thus far, or to go on alone.

At the moment of this first of the three scheduled stops along the way, at Dry Fork, Apache Wells and Lee's Ferry, the forces of respectability are comfortably in control. In a much-commented upon scene,[24] Ford subtly choreographs the movements of his characters round the table as the party are served a meal by Mrs Pickett. Ringo invites Dallas to sit at the table in a position close to that which Lucy has already assumed. We could at first interpret his action as that of a man for whom social conventions are irrelevant and social distinctions offensive. But more likely we read it as resulting from his gauche innocence, his ignorance of what is obvious to everyone else, that Dallas is a prostitute. Dallas, who knows full well what Lucy thinks of her, hesitates, but Ringo is persuasive. As she sits down there is no defiant glare from Ringo, who seems oblivious of Lucy's stare of disapproval. Hatfield with calculated rudeness offers Lucy a place at another table, nearer the window. Lucy is too well brought up to be quite as pointed in her rejection of Dallas as Hatfield, but not sufficiently emancipated from her social upbringing to stay seated next to a common whore. Ringo now confirms that he has no inkling of Dallas' offence by remarking, when Hatfield and Lucy have withdrawn, 'Looks like I got the plague, don't it?' Though Dallas mumbles, 'No, it's not you,' Ringo remains unaware of what has really happened,

Publicity shot of the scene at Dry Fork; (l. to r. standing) Donald Meek, Andy Devine, George Bancroft, Tim Holt, John Carradine, (seated) John Wayne, Claire Trevor, Louise Platt, Francis Ford, Berton Churchill, Thomas Mitchell

remarking philosophically, 'Well, I guess you can't break out of prison and into society in the same week.'

The delicacy of Ford's direction is striking: the tact with which he picks out the subtle gradations in feelings, from Hatfield's arrogant assumption of social superiority, to Lucy's evidence of a better nature, which has the courage to emerge only after Dallas has helped her give birth, to Dallas' pain, which she keeps to herself to spare both Ringo *and* Lucy embarrassment, and finally to Ringo's good-natured refusal to take offence. A natural democrat, confident of his own worth, he is indifferent to a snub.

This scene is the high point of the fortunes of the respectable sector of the party. From now on basic human qualities will count for far more than social position. The class consciousness which the snobs have tried to force upon the conduct of relations will become progressively eroded, reduced to irrelevance by the forces of nature as manifested in the Apache. Those who cannot accept egalitarianism, such as Hatfield or Gatewood, will perish or be removed from society.

XVII

The passage between Dry Fork and the next stop, Apache Wells, follows the established rhythm, cutting from long shots of the stage trundling along the lonely trail, to shots of Buck and Curly on top, to scenes inside the coach. Gatewood delivers his homily about the iniquity of regulating the banks, Hatfield snubs Dallas again by failing to offer her a drink from the silver cup he has given Lucy. Time passes; Doc Boone gets drunker and Dallas and Ringo develop their relationship through an exchange of significant glances.

As the stage drives into Apache Wells (also the name of a railroad station in Ford's *3 Godfathers*) it is greeted by four *vaqueros*. Chris, the owner of the little station, is a Mexican, played by Chris-Pin Martin, real name Ysabel Ponciana Chris-Pin Martin Piaz, who would provide comic relief in the 'Cisco Kid' series in the 1940s. Mexicans had fared ill in the early days of the Western. The word 'greaser' appears frequently in the titles of Westerns before 1920 – Francis Ford had a role in *Tony the Greaser* in 1911 – and there is a grossly caricatured Mexican villain in

John Ford's *Straight Shooting* in 1917. So prejudiced did the stereotype become that the Mexican government was moved to protest in the 1930s.

Stagecoach cannot be completely absolved of the casual racism of its time. The Hispanic heritage of the south-west is sketched in with some solidity – Luke Plummer has a Mexican side-kick, a detail not present in Nichols' script – but mostly by means of some stereotypical humour. The comic business about Buck's Mexican wife and the large number of her relations who expect to be fed is a joke Ford felt good enough to repeat about the characters played by Andy Devine in *Two Rode Together* and *The Man Who Shot Liberty Valance*. But it depends for its humour on a presumption that the audience 'knows' Mexicans are feckless and breed quickly.

Yet the film cunningly undercuts its own easy complicity in racist jibes. Chris is, stereotypically, overweight, not especially brave, and given to adding 'I theenk' to the end of every sentence. But he is kind to Lucy and concerned about the threat to Ringo in Lordsburg. And in a wonderful moment he turns the tables on the racism of the white passengers. Chris's wife is an Apache, and when Peacock sees her he rises in terror. 'She's savage!' he gasps. Chris's genuine incomprehension that his own wife could be the object of such ridiculous prejudice offers us a joke at Peacock's expense. 'Si, señor, she's a little bit savage, I theenk,' he replies, looking decidedly henpecked.

In the rather odd little scene which follows, Chris's wife Yakima (doubtless an in-joke to embarrass Canutt) sings a song in Spanish:

> Al pensar en tí
> Tierra en que nací
> Que nostalgia siente mi corazón
> En mi soledad
> Siento alivio y consuelo en mi dolor.
>
> Las notas tristes de esta canción
> Me traen recuerdos de aquel amor
> Al pensar en el
> Vuelve a renacer
> La alegria en mi triste corazón.

Top: Luke Plummer's Mexican side-kick
Bottom: Elvira Rios as Yakima

This translates as: 'When I think of you/Land where I was born/ Nostalgia fills my heart/In my solitude/This song/Brings relief and solace to my pain./The sad notes of this song/Bring me memories of that love/When I think of him/Once again happiness/Is reborn in my sad heart.' It's a plangent song of exile, in which a lament for the lost native land merges into a love song for an absent sweetheart. Yakima is played by Elvira Rios, a Mexican better known in her native land as a singer than as an actress, and whose only other Hollywood appearance was in *Tropic Holiday*, a Paramount Latin musical confection of 1938 featuring Tito Guizar. No sooner has Yakima finished her song than the four *vaqueros* make off with the spare horses, and by morning Yakima has gone too. For an Anglo audience, the song in Spanish is a reminder of the alien culture which surrounds the little island of 'civilisation' in the stage station, and for a brief moment the voice of the Other forces its way through. Whether Yakima's departure is motivated by a desire for her lost homeland or her thoughts of a lover we do not know, but her unseen departure adds to the threat which the passengers face. Chris had regarded her presence as insurance against Apache attack. Now he regrets her absence, but misses much more the horse and rifle she has taken. 'I can find another wife, easy, yes, but not a horse like that.' Ford was always more indulgent towards sexism than racism.

XVIII

In Ernest Haycox's original story, the army wife, who is nameless, is not pregnant. Haycox's Westerns were, one assumes, written for a largely male readership. The birth of Lucy's baby in *Stagecoach* seems expressly designed to give the film appeal to a more mixed audience. As we shall see, the studio publicity machine pitched several of its suggestions for promotional stunts at women spectators.

In terms of the mechanics of the plot, the baby provides the film with a dramatic crisis which substantially affects our view of most of the characters. It is Doc's big scene, in which he shows that through an effort of will power he is still able to perform professionally and gain respect. Dallas shows herself to be genuinely considerate towards others, even to those like Lucy who have scorned her, and she displays the proper maternal instincts that make her a fitting partner for Ringo, despite her past. Ringo, observing her true nature, is persuaded that he will marry her. Real concern for Lucy seems to break through Hatfield's cold, cynical exterior. Even Peacock comes into his own as an experienced family man who knows how to behave during a confinement ('Sh! Quiet!'). And Buck, who has been sublimely ignorant of Lucy's condition – despite his own large family the only one not to have guessed – manages to come up with a nickname for the new arrival: Little Coyote. Only Gatewood is unmoved, seeing in the miraculous birth only an inconvenience for himself. As Hatfield snaps at him, 'Why don't you think of anyone else for once?'

After the birth of the baby, there's a brief scene in which Ringo observes Dallas going outside for some air, and starts to join her until waylaid by Chris, who gives him the useful information that he has seen all three Plummers in Lordsburg. The scene is no more than a bridge between the previous one, in which the passengers digest the news of the baby's birth, and the following one, in which Ringo will finally declare his feeling for Dallas. In plot terms it does little more than further increase the suspense of the impending confrontation with the Plummers.

Even with a scene as minor as this Ford is incapable of merely going through the motions. Each scene, every shot is more than just functional to the narrative: there is always some added value. It may be a particular felicity of framing, or the subtlety with which the actors are blocked, or an elegant camera movement – Ford moves the camera so

Ringo with Chris

rarely that any movement has great effect. In the little scene with Ringo and Chris the pleasure comes from both framing and lighting, but mostly from the creation of a mood.

There are only two shots. The first, following the previous scene which had ended with Doc setting down his glass with a 'Phew!', has Ringo, screen left, leaning against the wall, looking down a dark corridor at the end of which is a lighted doorway. As he looks down the corridor, away from the camera, Dallas comes out of a doorway on the right and, without seeing Ringo, turns and walks off towards the door in long-shot. Ringo moves to follow her; the camera remains still, watching him walk away. As he gets halfway down the corridor, Chris comes out of a doorway to the left, carrying a lamp. Ringo stops to talk to him. Then there is a cut, to a two-shot of Chris and Ringo, Chris in profile on the left of the screen, Ringo on the right with his back to the camera, his face half turned towards Chris, catching the light. They speak. Ringo then bends to the lamp and lights his cigarette, the smoke shining white as it drifts through the lamplight. Ringo moves away, the camera steady as it watches him go out through the door.

There's a calm beauty in the scene which is in excess of the demands of the narrative, but not superfluous to our satisfaction as an audience. The two special pleasures of the scene, lighting and framing, both challenge the received wisdoms of film history. In the 1950s the great French critic André Bazin formulated a view of the history of film style which identified a decisive break at the start of the 1940s, with the development by such directors as Welles and Wyler of a shooting style based on deep focus. Whereas up to that point, asserted Bazin, a scene between two actors had usually been presented by the method of shot-reverse shot:

> It was this fashion of editing, so admirably suitable for the best films made between 1930 and 1939, that was challenged by the shot in depth introduced by Orson Welles and William Wyler. *Citizen Kane* can never be too highly praised. Thanks to depth of field, whole scenes are covered in one take, the camera remaining motionless.[25]

Bazin based a whole cinematic philosophy on the distinction between deep focus and the scene constructed by editing, believing that deep focus did less violence to the wholeness of physical space. True, Ford's scene does employ a cut. But the effect of the depth of field in the first shot – as Ringo watches Dallas but is not seen by her, turns briefly to see if the other passengers in the next room are observing him, then sets off after her only to be waylaid by Chris – is exactly as that practised by Welles and Wyler, deploying actors in movements to and from the camera instead of breaking up the scene into separate set-ups.

The lighting too anticipates what is usually considered a characteristic 1940s style. Low-key lighting effects, making highly deliberate use of strong shadows and chiaroscuro, are generally associated with the *film noir* style, customarily dated from *The Maltese Falcon* in 1941. Cigarette smoke caught in artificial light, ghostly white against deep shadows, became a trademark of *film noir*. The shot of Ringo and Chris conversing conspiratorially in hushed tones would fit easily into that genre, usually regarded as the very antithesis of the Western. And this use of low-key lighting is repeated through the entire last sequence in Lordsburg.

Ford's cameraman on *Stagecoach*, Bert Glennon, had worked for Sternberg on *Blonde Venus* and *The Scarlet Empress* and could be presumed to know a thing or two about lighting. Interviewed on the set of *Stagecoach* he was asked:

Q. – Other sets I have visited have many lights placed all around the top. I notice no parallel construction for lights on any of your sets and all of them have ceilings. Is that something new?

A. – Yes, it is a decided break from the conventional method of lighting sets and people. The ceilings were necessary because the sets were low, and as a certain reality of perspective is obtained by the use of the 25mm lens, which included ceiling in nearly every shot, the elimination of the conventional backlight or 'Hollywood halo' was forced. Believe me, it is quite difficult to obtain 'roundness' of image without the use of backlight, but in order to follow out the photographic idea, which was 'reproduce the method of lighting as used in the Sargent paintings of the early West', it was necessary to use backlight only when it was the source of the light.[26]

Someone is mistaken here. The standard reference work on the subject, *Samuels' Encyclopedia of Artists of the American West*, lists no artist under the name of Sargent.[27] One may speculate that Glennon had another artist in mind, Frederic Remington perhaps, whom Ford later admitted he had tried to copy in *She Wore a Yellow Ribbon*. Towards the end of his career Remington experimented with great success in the use of lighting effects in night scenes. At any rate it is clear that the lighting scheme of *Stagecoach* was highly deliberate. Glennon, who had shot Ford's previous success *The Hurricane*, went on to photograph the director's first colour film, *Drums Along the Mohawk* (1939), as well as other Ford Westerns such as *Wagon Master*, *Rio Grande* and *Sergeant Rutledge*.

Orson Welles' *Citizen Kane*, made in 1941, has been credited not only with the innovation of deep focus but also with the daring use of sets with ceilings. Welles himself frequently recalled that he had learned to be a director by watching Ford's films: 'John Ford was my teacher. My own style has nothing to do with his, but *Stagecoach* was my movie text-book. I ran it over forty times.'[28]

John Ford (left) with Bert Glennon (behind the camera)

XIX
. . . .

As always in a well-fashioned Hollywood script, each event serves not only to illuminate character but also to advance the narrative by triggering the next event. The birth of the baby deepens our knowledge of the dramatis personae. But it also precipitates a further crisis the next morning. In Doc's opinion, Lucy is too delicate to be moved. Once again there is a division between those who want to go on and those who advise delay or retreat. While this debate continues, Dallas, having summoned the courage to believe that she may have a chance with Ringo, seizes the opportunity to encourage him to escape.

Women in the Western represent the alternative to violence. Characteristically, the hero is faced with a choice: either he follows his code, which demands that he face physical danger and meet evil with force, or he chooses romance. What the woman offers is always the easy way out. She herself may be brave enough, but she represents the coward's option. The Western is constructed in such a way that the hero cannot choose what the woman offers and still live with himself. This stark choice is presented in its most schematic form in *High Noon*. Sheriff Gary Cooper's town is threatened by bad men. His wife is a Quaker. The equation of woman with non-violence could not be clearer: he must choose between her refusal of resistance and upholding the law. In the moral world of the West, civilisation depends on there being men who will not choose the seductive comforts the woman offers. A society without violence, a society fit for women, can only be established *through* violence.

For a moment Ringo appears to take the way out that Dallas shows him and opt for escape. She seems to have persuaded him that discretion is the better part of valour. He is poised to ride away from Curly, his jailer, away from the Plummers and away from what it is a man can't run away from. Fortunately for his status as hero, fate in the guise of the Apaches intervenes just in time. As he about to ride off he sees smoke signals rising from the distant hills. (Haycox's story begins: 'This was one of those years in the Territory when Apache smoke signals spiralled up from the stony mountain summits . . . ') So Ringo's decision that he must confront his nemesis in Lordsburg is made for him.

XX
....

Once again the coach is on the road. The journey until the next stop, Lee's Ferry, is brief. Dissent again breaks out between Hatfield and Gatewood, who is growing increasingly desperate through fear that further delays will deliver him into the hands of the law. Peacock attempts to pour oil on troubled waters: 'Let's have a little Christian charity, one for another.'

Strictly, the moral code of the Western hero is incompatible with Christianity. Ringo will emphatically not turn the other cheek. Yet the Christian overtones of *Stagecoach* are there for all to see. With an appropriateness that fiction could not better, the name of the actor playing Peacock is Meek. Blessed is he. The birth of the baby in what is, if not a stable then something close to it, echoes the Nativity story. (Ford twice filmed the Peter Kyne story 'Three Godfathers', an explicitly Christian parable.) Ford's Christianity is the only kind worth having, the radical Christianity of the New Testament, not the institutionalised Christianity of Popes and churches. In the true spirit of the Gospel, it is the outcasts – a prostitute, a drunk and an outlaw – who show charity, and who are redeemed. Those stained with the sin of pride, the haughty Hatfield and the hypocritical Gatewood, are damned.

XXI
....

The narrative of the film is carefully crafted, the tension constantly reinforced with new shocks and surprises. At Dry Fork the passengers are dismayed to learn that the army is not there to escort them further. At Apache Wells the birth of the baby adds to their problems, then the desertion of the Mexicans and Chris's Apache wife increases their sense of isolation. They believe that they will be safe once they reach Lee's Ferry – only to find the buildings burnt, the occupants killed and the ferry destroyed.

Ford does not make too much of the Apaches' depredations. There is a single shot of Hatfield, grim and silent, placing his coat over the half-naked body of a woman. This action is absent from Dudley Nichols' script, but in Haycox's story there are 'two nude figures

Above: Hatfield covers up Apache depredations
Overleaf: Fording the river

grotesquely bald, with deliberate knife slashes marking their bodies'. Haycox himself is restrained compared to the later fashion for rubbing our noses in the horrors of an Apache attack. An extreme example is Robert Aldrich's *Ulzana's Raid* (1972), in which a couple of warriors are seen to rip the heart out of a white victim and toss it back and forth like a football. (The scene was censored from prints released in Britain.)

After covering the woman's body, Hatfield looks up. In the distance we see the sun glinting on a hillside. As with the smoke signals Ringo has seen earlier, the audience, educated in the minutiae of the genre, needs no further sign that the Indian menace is still lurking. Curly organises some makeshift floats, logs lashed to the side, and the stage is driven across the river. There's one extraordinary shot from the opposite bank, with the sunlight streaming through the trees and sparkling on the spray thrown up by the plunging horses. The camera lingers just long enough for the effect to register, but not so long as to slow the narrative drive, which is now picking up tempo. Once across the river we are back in the desert (Monument Valley again), the music jaunty once more as Buck whips up the horses. Inside the coach there is a collective sigh of relief. Doc, drinking again now that his medical duties have been discharged, proposes a toast in which he even includes Gatewood. We know, with a certainty born of many such cinematic moments, that there is no time so dangerous as when tension has been relaxed. Barely has he raised the bottle to his lips than an arrow thuds through the window. The camera whips round to reveal the victim: the unfortunate Peacock, who topples forward with an apparently mortal wound.

XXII

The sequence of the chase is justly famous. It runs eight minutes 48 seconds, from the shot of Curly and Buck on the stage which precedes the pan across to Geronimo and his band, to the final dissolve into the town of Lordsburg. In that time there are 104 shots, giving an average shot length of five seconds. According to Tag Gallagher, the average shot length of the rest of the film is 10.5 seconds.[29] But it's not the sheer speed of the cutting that creates the excitement. The whole film has been building to this moment, constantly postponed yet always foreseen. The initial pan across Monument Valley shows the stage, small and vulnerable in the vast landscape, and then the Apache, much nearer. In the next shot they are nearer still. For the first time we see Geronimo in close-up, and then another Apache close too. Their faces are expressionless, which by convention we read as a sign of implacable cruelty. On the soundtrack the merrily-we-roll-along music changes abruptly to the minor chords which customarily introduce hostile Indians. After a further long shot of the valley and another pan across to the Apache, we revert to the occupants of the stage. These shots precede Doc Boone's toast, and so the arrival of the arrow has been well signposted.

The Indians come at them over a ridge, a couple of them falling under fire from the stage. At Curly's prompting Buck makes for the open space of the dry lake ahead. This they emerge onto by passing through a narrow defile in a shot which is an exact repeat of one which Ford made in *Straight Shooting* twenty-two years earlier. Ford chose not only the same location but the identical camera position. According to Rudy Behlmer, Ford had also used this location, the old wagon cut at Newhall, California, in *The Iron Horse* in 1924.[30] (In another example of recycling, Doc Boone's gesture at Apache Wells of throwing his whiskey in the fire after refusing to drink with Gatewood, thereby producing an explosive punctuation to the scene, is repeated nearly twenty years later by John Wayne in *The Searchers*.) Ford is either a very consistent or a very lazy film-maker. But who, shooting a Western

Left: Stagecoach (1939), right: Straight Shooting (1917)

in Hollywood in 1938, would suppose that fifty years later every shot would be put under the microscope?

Once out on the dry lake it's a furious chase as the Indians spread out on both sides of the coach and the passengers pour a fusillade of shots at them. The excitement generated by the action allows Ford to break with impunity one of the cardinal 'rules' of classical Hollywood cinema, the so-called 180-degree system. According to this convention, the space of any scene is constructed along an axis, the 180-degree line. In order to ensure that the audience maintains its bearings, its sense of where objects and people are in relation to each other, the camera shooting the scene must always stay on the same side of the line. Imagine a tennis match; if there is a camera on each side of the court and the director cuts each time a player makes a stroke, the ball will appear to be travelling always in the same direction. This violates the spectator's knowledge of the real space of the action.

According to accepted practice, the film director can sometimes get away with crossing the line, filming an action first from one side, then another, if each time the line is crossed there is a cut away to a close-up, or else to a head-on shot, in which the action is at right-angles to the line. This can distract from the apparent incongruity caused by crossing the line, and happens several times in the chase sequence. But Ford goes much further in breaking the rule. More than once he cuts directly from action going one way across the screen to a continuation of the same action going in the opposite direction. At one moment, for example, the stage is seen going from right to left, followed by the next

Crossing the line: consecutive shots of the stagecoach

shot in which it is speeding from left to right.

Of course it doesn't matter in the least that Ford breaks the rule. His audience, absorbed in the excitement of the scene, will be oblivious. Nor, one assumes, are most spectators bothered by the fact that many of the shots in the chase sequence were patently taken in the studio, with the stagecoach posed against a screen on to which were back-projected shots taken on location. It's pretty clear that none of the principal actors – with the exception of John Wayne – were ever at Muroc Dry Lake near Victorville, California, where the external shots were made, nor, indeed, at Monument Valley. Some location work did require the actors' presence. For example, John Carradine, Andy Devine, George Bancroft and Wayne are all clearly present when the scene of the stage crossing the river was filmed on the Kern River near Kernville, California. Other outdoor scenes, such as those at the other staging posts, also brought the actors out on location, being filmed in such places as Chatsworth and Calabasas, California. (All the interior scenes were shot on stages at the Goldwyn lot in Hollywood, as was the final confrontation between Ringo and the Plummers in Lordsburg. The opening scenes in Tonto were shot on the permanent Western street set at Republic Studios.)[31]

But if there is fakery in the matching of actors to the outdoor work, there is no cheating in the stunt-work. The remarkable stunt in which Ringo leaps from the speeding stage on to the first of the team of horses pulling it, then on to the second and finally on to the third, was performed by Yakima Canutt. *Stagecoach* was his first encounter with Ford. His contribution to the film was considerable. For the earlier scene of the stage crossing the river, Canutt devised an ingenious system of hollowed-out logs lashed to the coach's chassis and an underwater cable which pulled the conveyance across. His most difficult assignment in the picture was to play the Apache who jumps on to the leading horse of the stagecoach's team. According

Canutt (as Ringo) takes a leap

to Canutt's account in his autobiography, this 'transfer', as it is called in the trade, was performed at a speed of forty-five miles an hour as measured by the camera-car's speedometer.[32] Even though Canutt had a metal step fixed high on the horse's stirrup leather to enable him to get height on the jump, it was still a tricky thing to pull off. The second part of the stunt was even more dangerous. Once astride the leading horse Canutt as the Apache is shot by Ringo. We see him fall beneath the hooves of the horses, being dragged along as he holds on to the tongue of the rig until finally, in a single shot that guarantees the action is performed for real with no trickery, he lets go and the horses and the stage pass over him, the camera panning back to show him roll aside and climb slowly to his knees, as if wounded.

Since it wasn't something Canutt wanted to have to repeat, three cameras were used to ensure a good take – unusually for Ford. Unlike many Hollywood directors of the time, Ford didn't like to shoot a lot of 'cover', extra footage which could be juggled later in the cutting-room. His editor on *Stagecoach*, Dorothy Spencer, said: 'He cut in the camera.

Canutt's most difficult stunt

He got what he wanted on film, then left it to the cutter to put it together. Unlike most other directors, he never even went to the rushes. He left you alone to do your work. But if you did something he didn't like, he'd let you know about it.'[33]

Engrossing as the chase sequence is, some viewers have objected to an inherent implausibility. Ford himself recalled that Frank Nugent, who was later to write several of his films, said: 'Only thing I can't understand about it, Jack – in the chase, why didn't the Indians just shoot the horses pulling the stagecoach?' To which Ford replied: 'In actual fact that's probably what *did* happen, Frank, but if they had, it would have been the end of the picture, wouldn't it?'[34] In his autobiography *My Life East and West*, published just after *Stagecoach* was released, the veteran Western star W.S. Hart had made the same complaint. In one of his best-known paintings, 'Downing the Nigh Leader' (1907), Frederic Remington shows an Indian in the act of attacking the leading horses of a stagecoach team in full flight. But Ford was never unduly troubled by pedantic intrusions from real life.

XXIII

....

Nor was he afraid of patently melodramatic effects. The last-minute rescue of the passengers by the cavalry, after their ammunition has run out, had been a cliché in the cinema at least since D.W. Griffith used it in *The Battle at Elderbush Gulch* in 1913. Ford seems always to have had confidence in his ability to find a fresh way of presenting familiar situations. So instead of simply cross-cutting between the beleaguered travellers and the approaching cavalry, the camera remains on Lucy Mallory as she prepares with prayer for inevitable death, and then records the slow dawning across her face that a bugle is blowing in the distance. We see the recognition that salvation is at hand before we ourselves realise what the music on the soundtrack portends. As always with Ford, it's not the events in themselves which are of importance; it's their effect on the emotions of his characters which moves us. In a similar way, we hear the cries of the new-born baby and register the feelings of the passengers before we see it for ourselves.

Frederic Remington, 'Downing the Nigh Leader', 1907

The one fatality of the attack is suffered at the very moment of rescue. In a close-up we see Hatfield break open his revolver to reveal just one bullet left. He advances the chamber to the firing position and puts the gun to Lucy's head. His intention is to preserve her from that fate worse than death which Victorian melodrama knew so well. The trained audience needs no explanation of his action or of his motive. Like the cavalry rescue, they can be traced back in the cinema at least as far as *The Battle at Elderbush Gulch*, and in other art forms a good deal further. The dread of capture by Indians was etched deeply and early into the white American mind. Captivity narratives, stories of the tribulations of whites taken by Indians, date back to the seventeenth century, to the publication in 1682 of the story of Mary Rowlandson's capture during King Philip's War. Though many stories of male captives were published, it is the threat of sexual violation of the white woman by the male of another race which gave many of these tales their special frisson. Sexual relations between white women and their Indian captors are at the heart of two later Ford Westerns, *The Searchers*

The last bullet

and *Two Rode Together.* Hatfield, as the representative of Southern chivalry, is the most appropriate character to 'save' Lucy. And he it is, we remember, who has seen at close hand the fate meted out to the woman at Lee's Ferry and has covered her body with his coat. But he may be appropriate also because his heightened sensitivity to the danger of violation can be viewed as a displaced echo of Southern fears of the sexual 'threat' of the blacks.

XXIV

The removal of the Indian threat leaves much business to be resolved. Question marks still hang over the fates of four of the characters. Lucy does not know if her husband, reported wounded at Apache Wells, is alive or dead. Gatewood is a criminal on the run; will he escape justice? Ringo, also on the run, seeks to resolve his feud with the Plummers. And Dallas must wait to see if Ringo's apparent commitment to her will survive knowledge of her true circumstances.

Lucy's story is concluded first. Her husband is alive and well, and she is hustled away by Lordsburg's equivalent of the Law and Order League, one of whom fixes Dallas with the look she has come to know too well. But not before Lucy acknowledges her debt to Dallas. For Ford, it's never too late to repent.

Peacock, wounded in the Indian attack, is taken away on a stretcher. Dallas says goodbye affectionately, and for one final time the joke is repeated: 'Mr – uh?' – 'Peacock,' replies the whiskey drummer, resigned forever to repeating his name to those who have mislaid it. Gatewood is soon taken care of. The local marshal comes forward with a pair of handcuffs he intends for Ringo. But when Gatewood identifies himself, he finds, rather like Dr Crippen, that the telegraph has got there before him, and he is marched off to jail, still blustering. (There's a slight confusion in the plotting here. Gatewood clearly does not know about the telegraph wires being cut when he leaves Tonto, since he claims to have had a telegram from Lordsburg – a mystery which exercises Curly for most of the trip. When the sheriff of Lordsburg arrests him, he taunts Gatewood: 'You didn't think they'd have the telegraph wires fixed, did you?' Obviously if he didn't know they were cut he wouldn't know they were fixed. But also, if he didn't know they were cut when he left, why wasn't he afraid news of his theft would precede him to Lordsburg?)

Gatewood's arrest clears the decks for the final confrontation between Ringo and the Plummers. Luke has been discovered in the saloon, playing cards. He is dealt a hand of aces and eights, the 'dead man's hand' – a superstition dating back to Wild Bill Hickok, dealt just such a hand immediately prior to being shot in the back by Jack McCall in Deadwood in 1876. Hatfield, toying with a pack of cards at the table while the passengers were stopped at Dry Fork, had turned up an ace of spades. He too will not survive.

Tom Tyler as Luke looks a match for Ringo: tall, tough, wearing bat-wing chaps and several days' growth of beard – in the days before designer stubble, an infallible sign of a bad man. But before Ringo can face him in the street, Dallas has her own confrontation, has to let Ringo know who and what she is. He escorts her to her house, through a red-light area of honky-tonk houses with tinkling pianos, outside

Aces and eights

which loiter a motley group of gaudily dressed women and their customers. 'Don't come any further,' Dallas cries, unable to bear her shame. We can't be sure whether Ringo is still innocently unaware that she is a prostitute, or whether he simply doesn't care. But if he survives the Plummers he will come back for her.

The ritual confrontation of adversaries in the street, the Western variant on the eighteenth-century duel, is a stock narrative device that predates the cinema. Frederic Remington, who codified so many of the images that became part of the Western's repertoire, did the illustrations for Theodore Roosevelt's *Ranch Life and the Hunting Trail*, published in 1896. One of Remington's pictures is entitled 'A Fight in the Street'. It shows two men with pistols drawn, blazing away at each other outside a saloon. Owen Wister's novel *The Virginian*, first published in 1902, endowed the embryonic Western with narrative coherence and cultural respectability. It culminates in a fight in the street between its eponymous hero and the villain, Trampas. Wister's description of the actual shooting is pared down to the minimum:

Frederic Remington, 'A Fight in the Street', 1896

A wind seemed to blow his sleeve off his arm, and he replied to it, and saw Trampas pitch forward. He saw Trampas raise his arm from the ground and fall again, and lie there this time, still. A little smoke was rising from the pistol on the ground, and he looked at his own, and saw the smoke flowing upward out of it.

Terseness is a tradition in the Western, in which loquaciousness is often associated with effeminacy. The visual equivalent is the extreme economy with which Ford shoots the fight. As Ringo and the three Plummer brothers advance towards each other from opposite ends of the darkened street, we see Ringo in a low-angle shot take five steps forward, each marked by a resounding chord on the soundtrack, and suddenly drop to the ground. As he does so he shoots. We cut immediately to Dallas, standing waiting while more shots are fired. As with the cavalry rescue, the crucial action takes place off-screen, while we see the emotion on a woman's face. Only when Luke Plummer walks with an unnaturally steady gait into the saloon and falls dead on the floor do we know the outcome.

The 'spaghetti Western' of the 1960s was a highly self-conscious pastiche of the Hollywood original. From the first, Sergio Leone and his epigones set out to construct works that deliberately play with the conventions of the American Western, rather than slavishly imitate them. Sometimes the spaghettis parody by isolating a characteristic and exaggerating it. The taciturnity of The Man With No Name is a *reductio ad absurdum* of the 'yep' and 'nope' vocabulary of the Gary Cooper manner. At other times the Italians took things to the opposite extreme. In *A Fistful of Dollars* and the films that followed, the gunfights are stretched out to an inordinate degree, deliberately transgressing against the spareness of the *Stagecoach* style.

Ringo's dispatch of the Plummers is almost mythic in its efficiency, believable only because we don't actually witness it. After it is over he returns to give himself up to Curly. But the marshal doesn't have the heart to take him back to jail. With Dallas already up on the seat, he hands the reins of the buggy to Ringo and smacks the horse's rump to send them on their way. 'Well, they're saved from the blessings of civilisation,' says Doc Boone: not only the Doc's own personal judgment on the society which has made him an outcast but also Ford's final verdict on respectability. Curly then offers him a drink. 'Just one,' Doc replies. Some have read this as a sign that his experiences have matured him to the point of sobriety. This is unconvincing, not just because it flies in the face of the Fordian view of drinking, not just because it ignores the twinkle in Doc's eye when he says it, but because it assumes Doc is willing to enter into that very state of respectability from which he is celebrating the escape of Dallas and Ringo.

The film ends, as all good Westerns do, with the hero riding off away from the camera towards the distant horizon – but not alone like Shane. The Western hero as inveterate loner is an invention of the post-war period, when the Western's age of innocence was over and the hero had existential burdens to bear.

XXV
....

Stagecoach took forty-seven working days to shoot, completing photography on 23 December 1938. In those days post-production was speedy. The finished film was ready for preview at the Fox Westwood theatre on 2 February 1939. As a result of the audience reaction a cut was made to a scene which takes place soon after Ringo has joined the coach. Doc Boone has alleged that Hatfield has shot a man in the back. A fight looks likely, so Peacock suggests the party join him in hymn singing. But instead Doc launches into the old Western classic 'Ten Thousand Cattle Gone Astray', and one by one the party join in.[35] Ford eventually got to use this song in *My Darling Clementine* seven years later, when Chihuahua sings it to Wyatt Earp.

Stagecoach was released a month later, on 2 March 1939. Following the usual practice of the day, a pressbook was produced for exhibitors, full of ideas for exploiting the film's appeal. Posters were obtainable publicising the film as the latest production of a top director ('The director of *The Hurricane* now gives you lusty excitement and roaring adventure') and the newest work of its eminent producer ('Walter Wanger, producer of *Trade Winds* and *Algiers*, makes only six pictures a year, concentrating on making each one unusual, outstanding. That's why – a Wanger picture is always worth seeing'). The film was also, rather oddly, sold on its suspense, as if it were a kind of Hitchcockian thriller:

THE DIRECTOR OF
"THE HURRICANE"
NOW GIVES YOU
LUSTY EXCITEMENT
AND ROARING
ADVENTURE . . . . . . John Ford,
Academy Award
winner who made
'The Informer" and
'Submarine Patrol,
has packed sus-
pense into his new-
est picture. It's as
big as the wide
horizon of the
plains!

WALTER WANGER presents

STAGECOACH

with **CLAIRE TREVOR** • **JOHN WAYNE**

Andy Devine • John Carradine • Thomas Mitchell • Louise
Platt • George Bancroft • Donald Meek • Berton Churchill • Tim Holt
RELEASED THRU UNITED ARTISTS

THEATRE

Poster for *Stagecoach*

> The West as it really was! Nine oddly assorted strangers start by stagecoach for Lordsburg, New Mexico. Each has his own personal reasons for wanting to get there. Then strange things begin to happen. ... Courage and cowardice, love and hate come startlingly to the surface. ... (Due to the tremendous suspense developed in *Stagecoach*, we recommend that you get to the theatre for the start of the picture.)

Much play is made in the pressbook of the film's authenticity. 'Breathtaking Realism,' screams one poster. Indians from a reservation near Kayenta, Arizona are said to have 'revived their almost forgotten arts to aid in the production. Chief among these was smoke-signaling and coded rock messages ... ' The Lordsburg set is claimed to be a faithful reproduction of the town as it actually was in the 1880s. 'In order to create authentic sets for *Stagecoach* technicians not only delved into many volumes but also traveled hundreds of miles and interviewed dozens of pioneers in Arizona and New Mexico.' The stagecoach used is, we are reliably informed, an original Concord model. The costumes and hairstyles worn by the women, though authentically of the era when the film is set, lack nothing in appeal to the contemporary female audience:

> While Miss America is dashing to the smartest shops and the swankiest hairdressers to have her shapely self draped with the very latest in clothing and to have her hair 'upswept', she is actually purchasing 1885 styles. This revelation is made by Thelma Courtermarsh of the wardrobe department at the Walter Wanger Studio where *Stagecoach*, a frontier drama, was recently completed. Her statement is substantiated by Walter Plunkett, famous Hollywood costumer, who designed the dresses, and by Carmen Derigo, who arranged the coiffure Claire Trevor wears in her scenes. ... it was difficult to make her look old fashioned because the 1885 hair style is pin for pin with the modern high 'hair do'.

As confirmation of the tie-in with contemporary fashion, the pressbook shows the newspaper advertisement which Max Factor produced for Tru-Color Lipstick, backed by a picture of Claire Trevor highlighting

MAX FACTOR ADS TIE WITH TREVOR, PLATT

CLAIRE TREVOR
in Walter Wanger's
"STAGECOACH"

JOHN FORD
Production

SPECIAL ENGAGEMENT

MAX FACTOR MAKE-UP ARTIST

★ Here is your opportunity to
learn the exact shades of make-
up most becoming to your type.

FREE...Your
complexion
analysis and
color harmony
make-up chart.

Max Factor's
TRU-COLOR LIPSTICK $1.00

MAX FACTOR MAKE-UP SERVICE DEPT...MAIN FLOOR

Max Factor Ltd. through fine cosmetic counters everywhere, has tied up with Claire Trevor and Louise Platt in newspaper advertising copy promoting one of its products. The copy gives credit to " Stagecoach," and will be inserted in newspapers on a schedule timed with your showing. Watch your local papers for the ads, and co-operate with local Max Factor dealers by promoting displays tying in with the showing of " Stagecoach " at your theatre. For the name of your local dealer contact:

J. P. McKenna
MAX FACTOR LTD.,
16 Old Bond Street,
London, W.1

Top: Max Factor ad.
Bottom: Claire Trevor's 'modern high hair-do'

Stagecoach. The pressbook gives details of a full range of promotional products which exhibitors could send for, including bookmarks and novelty Western hats (17 cents apiece). The film was translated into other media for dissemination via a variety of publicity channels. There was a 15–minute disc available to radio stations, a 5,000–word newspaper serialisation, a photo-story version also for newspapers, and the script of a 15–minute dramatisation intended for performance in schools. ('*Stagecoach* offers you a number of high-powered angles for selling the picture through the schools – angles that no showman will want to miss because of their sure profit and good-will returns!')

No angle was left unexplored. ('Find an old-timer who lived in your town or had some connection with the stagecoach route during that time, and bring him in on a big blast of showmanship for the picture.') Though some of the stunts suggested sound too corny for even the most enthusiastic showman, the trade journals record that many of the ideas were indeed taken up. The *Motion Picture Herald* for 25 March 1939 shows the Mayor of Boston handing a letter to the driver of a stagecoach for delivery to the Mayor of Providence, R.I. In Indianapolis, recorded the *Herald* on 15 April, a stagecoach picked up mail from the airport, where it was posed for local newspapers against an aeroplane. And on 20 May the *Herald* reported: 'Material that had been used by the Boy Scouts at the Washington Jamboree in 1937 was taken out of the mothballs and used for street bally by Bill Smith for the *Stagecoach* date at the Palace in Breckenridge, Tex. Tepees, drums, fireplace, etc., were set up in front of theatre ahead and during run, with Boy Scouts dressed as Indians with headgear and bows and arrows stationed on guard.'

XXVI
....

The pressbook also contained ready-made reviews for use by local papers whose film critics lacked confidence in their own judgment. Helpfully providing a blank space into which the name of the local theatre could be dropped, one review begins:

With a cast studded with brilliant stars, and a story of breathless speed and excitement, *Stagecoach* rode into the ...... Theatre last night for its local premiere. ... *Stagecoach* has the advantages of an excellent screenplay by Dudley Nichols, masterful direction by John Ford, and the usual place [pace?] and authenticity that distinguish a Walter Wanger production.

For once the verdicts of the genuine critics were no less enthusiastic than the pre-packaged reviews. In the *New York Times* of 3 March 1939 Frank S. Nugent, later to script *Fort Apache* and other Westerns for Ford, wrote:

John Ford has swept aside ten years of artifice and talkie compromise and has made a motion picture that sings a song of camera. It moves, and how beautifully it moves, across the plains of Arizona, skirting the sky-reaching mesas of Monument Valley, beneath the piled-up cloud banks which every photographer dreams about ...

Mr Ford is not one of your subtle directors, suspending sequences on the wink of an eye or the precisely calculated gleam of a candle in a mirror. He prefers the broadest canvas, the brightest colors, the widest brush and the boldest possible strokes. He hews to the straight narrative line with the well-reasoned confidence of a man who has seen that narrative succeed before. He takes no shadings from his characters; either they play it straight or they don't play at all. He likes his language simple and he doesn't want too much of it. When his Redskins bite the dust, he expects to hear the thud and see the dirt spurt up. Above all, he likes to have things happen in the open, where his camera can keep them in view. ... This is one stagecoach that's powered by a Ford.

The trade papers were equally enthusiastic. A month before, on 8 February 1939, *Variety* had in its familiar staccato style called the picture a 'sweeping and powerful drama of the American frontier' which 'displays potentialities that can easily drive it through as one of the surprise big grossers of the year. Without strong marquee names, picture nevertheless presents wide range of exploitation to attract, and will carry far through word-of-mouth after it gets rolling. Directorially, production is John Ford in peak form.' The *Motion Picture Herald* of 11 February rated the film 'a solid and soundly satisfying demonstration of the virtue inherent in the entertainment-for-entertainment's-sake policy of film production ... gripping in universal appeal, spectacular in photographic beauty.' *Photoplay* (4 April 1939) called it 'Grand Hotel on wheels' and was full of praise for Wayne's 'attractive and sincere' performance. In Britain, then the biggest single foreign market for Hollywood films, the response was equally positive. *Film Weekly* on 10 June called it 'a perfect blend of humanity and suspense ... absolutely first class.' Prophetically, it remarked: 'Should mark [John Wayne's] escape from minor Westerns into something more worthy of his virile performance in this practically perfect picture.' A. Jympson Harman in the *Evening News* (9 June 1939) was likewise prescient: 'This is a great film – the kind that gets itself into the movie history books.' It appealed equally to female reviewers. C.A. Lejeune in the *Observer* (11 June 1939) called it 'One of the most exciting experiences the cinema has brought us,' a view echoed by Dilys Powell in the *Sunday Times* (11 June 1939): 'One of the most exciting Westerns I have seen for years.'

This chorus of praise was consolidated by the prestigious New York Critics Best Director award to Ford. The National Board of Review voted the film the year's third best. It did not do so well in the Academy Awards. 1939 was something of an *annus mirabilis* for Hollywood, with the release of *Mr Smith Goes to Washington*, *The Wizard of Oz*, *Only Angels Have Wings*, *Ninotchka*, *Goodbye, Mr Chips*, *The Roaring Twenties* and of course *Gone With the Wind*. The latter cleaned up most of the Oscars. But as well as an Oscar for Best Musical Score, *Stagecoach* was recognised with an Oscar for Thomas Mitchell as Best Supporting Actor.

XXVII

....

Stagecoach was a success at the box office too. The Played and Earned records of United Artists show the gross monthly earnings during 1939 as follows:

	$
February	9,445.73
March	168,507.32
April	260,810.44
May	300,092.29
June	114,998.68
July	47,369.55
August	22,596.59
September	13,109.04
October	8,065.18
November	8,281.73
December	3,651.36
TOTAL	956,927.91

During that period the picture also earned $48,358.15 in Canada. Earnings overseas are not recorded. (The earnings of $9,445.73 for the month of February indicate that although the official release was not till 2 March, some exhibition activity took place in advance of that date.) According to the records, the producer's share of these sums was 75%, i.e. $753,964.65, a respectable return on Wanger's initial investment of $531,374.13, even without foreign earnings.[36]

It has been claimed that *Stagecoach* revived the fortunes of the Western, which had been in the doldrums since the beginning of the decade. The production of A-Westerns, with big budgets and major stars, had certainly slumped in the mid-1930s, slipping down to zero in 1934 and rising only to four in 1938. 1939 did see a revival, with the release of major Western features from several studios. 20th Century-Fox came out with *Jesse James*, starring Tyrone Power as the notorious train-robber. Cecil B. DeMille directed *Union Pacific* for Paramount, with Barbara Stanwyck and Joel McCrea, and Warner Bros. produced *Dodge City* with Errol Flynn and *The Oklahoma Kid*, starring James Cagney and Humphrey Bogart. Other major Westerns followed later in the year: Allan Dwan's *Frontier Marshal* with Randolph Scott, *Destry Rides Again* with James Stewart and Marlene Dietrich, and Ford's own *Drums Along the Mohawk*.

Most of these films would have been in production too soon to have been directly affected by the success of *Stagecoach*, and its effect on later productions was probably not decisive. Browsing through the *Motion Picture Herald*, one can see that the sheer promotional muscle put behind both *Dodge City* and *Jesse James* far outweighed what *Stagecoach* could command. This is reflected in full-colour advertising and announcements of extravagant promotional jamborees. Warners and Fox had much greater clout in the industry than United Artists, not least because of the numbers of first-run movie theatres which they owned. UA, an umbrella sheltering a group of talented but maverick independents, had no theatres of its own. The fact that the total of A-Westerns produced in 1940 shot up to thirteen probably owed more to the solid commercial success which Warners and Fox achieved with their films than to Wanger's unexpected, if deserved, hit.

XXVIII
....

In the fifty years since the first reviews of *Stagecoach* appeared, its status of undisputed classic, achieved almost overnight, has never been seriously challenged. But Ford's reputation generally has known its ups and downs. Within the industry and among the film-going public his stock was higher than it had ever been in the years following *Stagecoach*, with Oscars for *The Grapes of Wrath* in 1940 and for *How Green Was My Valley* in 1941. But his work in the later 1940s and in the 50s seemed to disappoint those critics who valued Ford as a prestige director of important and weighty subjects. What on earth, they thought, was the director of *The Informer* doing wasting his time on such bizarre confections as *When Willie Comes Marching Home* or *The Sun Shines Bright*, or on run-of-the-mill Westerns like *Rio Grande*?

In France, Ford continued to be appreciated, and not just for his arty films. Jean Mitry in his study *John Ford*, published in 1954, groups *Stagecoach* together with *The Grapes of Wrath* and *The Long Voyage Home* in a chapter entitled 'Three Masterpieces'. He praises *Stagecoach* particularly for its subtlety of rhythm, the relationship between the exterior shots of the stage on its journey and the interior shots of the drama inside. These are, says Mitry, 'like two fugues which react together in a contrapuntal effect, increasingly tightened.'[37]

Also in France, André Bazin writing in the early 1950s placed

Stagecoach at the zenith of what he identified as the 'classical' Western:

> In seeing again today such films as *Jezebel* by William Wyler,
> *Stagecoach* by John Ford, or *Le Jour se lève* by Marcel Carné, one
> has the feeling that in them art has found its perfect balance, its
> ideal form of expression, and reciprocally one admires them for
> dramatic and moral themes to which the cinema, while it may
> not have created them, has given a grandeur, an artistic
> effectiveness, that they would otherwise not have had. In short,
> here are all the characteristics of the ripeness of a classical art.[38]

In another essay Bazin developed his notion that *Stagecoach* represented
the pinnacle of classicism, contrasting it with the Westerns of the post-
war era:

> By the eve of the war the Western had reached a definitive stage
> of perfection. The year 1940 marks a point beyond which some
> new development seemed inevitable, a development that the four
> years of war delayed, then modified, though without controlling
> it. *Stagecoach* (1939) is the ideal example of the maturity of a style
> brought to classical perfection. John Ford struck the ideal balance
> between social myth, historical reconstruction, psychological
> truth and the traditional theme of the Western *mise en scène*. None
> of these elements dominated any other. *Stagecoach* is like a wheel,
> so perfectly made that it remains in equilibrium on its axis in any
> position.[39]

After the war, Bazin maintained, a mutation set in, a development
towards something he called the 'superwestern': 'a Western that would
be ashamed to be just itself, and looks for some additional interest to
justify its existence – an aesthetic, sociological, moral, psychological,
political or erotic interest, in short some quality extrinsic to the genre
and which is supposed to enrich it.' Bazin cites *Duel in the Sun, High
Noon* and *Shane* as examples of this tendency, all films which in his view
add something extra to the Western which was not there in its original
state of innocence.

Ford's own post-war Westerns do not, perhaps, fit neatly into

Bazin's category of 'superwestern'. And though there is undeniably a darker tone observable in several of them, especially in those of the later 50s and 60s such as *The Searchers, Sergeant Rutledge* and *Two Rode Together*, these were not the Ford films most favoured by his foremost British champion, Lindsay Anderson. In his monograph on Ford – originally written for the British Film Institute in the early 1950s, but revised and expanded for publication in 1981 – Anderson favoured Ford the lyrical poet of *She Wore a Yellow Ribbon* and *The Quiet Man* over the self-conscious artist of *The Informer*. This view, once heretical, is now the dominant one. (His book contains a fascinating, though fiercely contentious, account of Ford and the critics.) Yet for all that, his appreciation of *Stagecoach* is muted. He writes that 'its excellence is the excellence of masterly narrative prose, taut, dynamic, and irresistibly holding. These virtues are of course characteristic of Ford – the swinging rhythm, the broad landscapes, the hectic excitement of the chase across the flats – but the very urgency of the drive leaves little room for the more intimate revelations of style.'[40] This is faint praise indeed from such a Ford enthusiast.

In his preface Anderson calls Ford 'probably the greatest film director working in the world's richest film-making tradition', but this was not the received view in the 1950s.[41] Since 1952 *Sight and Sound* has conducted a poll every decade to find the ten films most rated by film critics worldwide. No Ford film made the top ten in 1952, nor in 1962. Nor did Ford make the list of top ten directors, first introduced in 1962. In that year came the first issue of the iconoclastic magazine *Movie*, with its now notorious 'talent histogram', in which the young Turks of British film criticism consigned British and American directors to their allotted places. Only two directors were rated 'great': Hitchcock and Hawks. Ford did not even make the next grade, that of the merely 'brilliant', which comprised Cukor, Donen, Mann, McCarey, Minnelli, Preminger, Ray, Sirk, Tourneur, Walsh and Welles. Instead, he squeezed into the third category, that of the 'very talented'. By 1972, however, Ford had climbed to sixth place in the *Sight and Sound* directors list, and *The Searchers* made joint seventeenth place. In 1982 Ford rose to fourth in the directors list, and *The Searchers* just made the top ten. If *Sight and Sound*'s little game continues in 1992, it's worth a bet that Ford will climb another place or two and *The Searchers* will further improve on its rating.

Ford's rise up the *Sight and Sound* poll in 1972 reflects the moves to rehabilitate his reputation in the later 1960s. In a landmark article on Ford in *New Left Review* in 1965, Peter Wollen provided an admirably concise account of the essence of the director's work. Andrew Sarris' *The American Cinema*, published in 1968, employed, rather like *Movie*, a hierarchical ranking system as a means of mapping the entire field of Hollywood cinema. But, reversing the judgment of *Movie*, Sarris placed Ford in the top category of 'Pantheon Directors'. In 1976 Sarris published a book-length study, *The John Ford Movie Mystery*. For Sarris, the value of *Stagecoach* is seen to reside in its personal style, in its Fordian-ness, as it were. Characteristic of the Fordian effect is the 'double image, alternating between close-ups of emotional intimacy and long shots of epic involvement, thus capturing both the twitches of life and the silhouettes of legend.'[42] Two years before Sarris' book, Joseph McBride and Michael Wilmington had published their own book-length study of the director's work. In it they offered a slightly tongue-in-cheek interpretation of *Stagecoach* as a political parable:

> The coach is America, a nation of exiles, riven with warring and contradictory factions; the Indians are the wild forces of nature; the pregnant woman is Liberty; the banker is the corrupt Republican Establishment, the spokesman for selfish individualism; the benevolent sheriff riding shotgun is Roosevelt; the Plummer Gang are the Axis powers; Buck, the driver, and his Mexican wife 'Hoolietta' are the ethnic mixtures which give the country its democratic character.[43]

But the value of the film, say McBride and Wilmington, lies not in its historical significance but in 'the vividness with which it creates a dream landscape from the American past and peoples it with simple and striking characters who, despite their reincarnation in countless 'A' and 'B' Westerns, still retain a believable ambivalence and depth.'[44]

Ford's status in the pantheon has recently been confirmed by the critical biography by Tag Gallagher, *John Ford: The Man and his Films*, which appeared in 1986. But Gallagher's enthusiasm for Ford's best-known film is less than whole-hearted. He calls it 'too self-conscious to revive completely the earthy intimacy' of Ford's early silent films, 'while its mixture of artfulness and commerciality set it apart from the Argosy Westerns too'[45] such as *Fort Apache* and *3 Godfathers*. In company with virtually all contemporary critics, Gallagher rates Ford's later Westerns such as *The Searchers* and *The Man Who Shot Liberty Valance* as greater works.

Yet if the critical consensus today does not place *Stagecoach* among the greatest of Ford's films, in the popular mind it rates not just as a classic, but as *the* classic Western, according to Brian Henderson.[46] On its fiftieth anniversary in 1989 the US Post Office put *Stagecoach* on a stamp, along with *The Wizard of Oz*, *Beau Geste* and *Gone With the Wind*. For Bazin, its classic status has to do with its perfect balance of the social and the psychological. *Stagecoach*, too, is a supreme example of the mature aesthetic of so-called 'classical' Hollywood cinema, in which story, character, location, and the formal elements of lighting, framing, editing are all in harmony. It was created on the cusp of the long wave that had been building since the feature film had emerged nearly twenty-five years before, and which, according to Bazin, would break a mere two years later, tumbling the cinema into a more turbulent era. But for Ford himself and for Merian Cooper in their dispute with Selznick, 'classic' meant something more immediate, meant it would have class – as *Hollywood Reporter* astutely put it, 'One swellegant Western that even the carriage trade will go for'.[47] A film that would not be a Western at all in the limited industry meaning of the term, all action and no talk, a shoot 'em up, but rather a film of universal and perennial appeal. About that they have been proved right.

Two Navaho extras take a lunch break

NOTES

· ·

1 See her entry on 'Costume' in *The BFI Companion to the Western*, ed. Edward Buscombe (London: BFI/André Deutsch, 1988).

2 Gorham Kindem, 'Hollywood's Conversion to Color', in Gorham Kindem (ed.), *The American Movie Industry* (Carbondale: Southern Illinois University Press, 1982), p. 152.

3 Quoted in Ronald Haver, *David O. Selznick's Hollywood* (London: Secker & Warburg, 1980), p. 224.

4 See *Motion Picture Herald*, 7 January 1939. In the same issue Columbia's *Stagecoach Days*, 58 minutes long, starring Jack Luden and Eleanor Stewart, plus 'Tuffy (a dog)', *is* listed as a Western.

5 Rudy Behlmer (ed.), *Memo From David O. Selznick* (New York: Avon Books, 1972), p. 155.

6 *Memo From David O. Selznick*, p. 156.

7 Tino Balio, *United Artists: The Company Built by the Stars* (Madison: University of Wisconsin Press, 1976), p. 138.

8 Kindem, p. 153.

9 State Historical Society of Wisconsin, Walter Wanger Papers, Box 93, folder 7.

10 Tag Gallagher, *John Ford: The Man and his Films* (Berkeley: University of California Press, 1986). p.12.

11 In his entry on *Stagecoach* in *The BFI Companion to the Western*.

12 See Fred Balshofer and Arthur C. Miller, *One Reel a Week* (Berkeley: University of California Press, 1967), p. 80.

13 Quoted in William E. Leuchtenburg, *Franklin D. Roosevelt and the New Deal* (New York: Harper & Row, 1963), p. 22.

14 Gallagher, p. 342.

15 Gallagher, p. 465.

16 Rudy Behlmer, *America's Favorite Movies* (New York: Frederick Ungar, 1982), p. 106.

17 The reference to Billy Pickett is pointed out by Jean-Louis Leutrat and Suzanne Liandrat-Guigues, *Les Cartes de l'Ouest* (Paris: Armand Colin, 1990), p. 149.

18 Peter Bogdanovich, *John Ford* (London: Studio Vista, 1967), p. 69.

19 Bogdanovich, p. 69.

20 Maurice Zolotow, *Shooting Star: A Biography of John Wayne* (New York: Simon & Schuster, 1974).

21 Todd McCarthy, 'John Ford and Monument Valley', *American Film*, May 1978.

22 Gallagher, p. 341.

23 *America's Favorite Movies*, p. 117.

24 By, for example, Nick Browne in 'The Spectator-in-the-Text: The Rhetoric of *Stagecoach*', *Film Quarterly*, Winter 1975; Tag Gallagher in *John Ford: The Man and his Films*, p. 159; J.-L. Leutrat and S. Liandrat-Guigues, *Les Cartes de l'Ouest*, p. 164f.

25 André Bazin, 'The Evolution of the Language of Cinema' in Hugh Gray (trans.) *What is Cinema?* (Berkeley: University of California Press, 1967), p. 33.

26 Interviewed in *American Cinematographer*, February 1939.

27 Peggy and Harold Samuels, *Samuels' Encyclopedia of Artists of the American West* (Secaucus, N.J.: Castle, 1985).

28 Quoted in Gallagher, p. 152.

29 Gallagher, p. 153.

30 *America's Favorite Movies*, p. 112.

31 *America's Favorite Movies*, p. 114.

32 Yakima Canutt, *Stunt Man* (New York: Walker and Company, 1979), p. 110.

33 Quoted in *Action*, September–October 1971.

34 Bogdanovich, p. 72.

35 *America's Favorite Movies*, p. 117.

36 'Played and Earned: *Stagecoach*, picture no. 456', State Historical Society of Wisconsin, Walter Wanger Papers, Box 93, folder 7.

37 Jean Mitry, *John Ford* (Paris: Editions Universitaires, 1954), p. 71.

38 Bazin, 'The Evolution of the Language of Cinema', p. 29.

39 Bazin, 'The Evolution of the Western', in Hugh Gray (trans.), *What is Cinema? Vol. II* (Berkeley: University of California Press, 1971), p. 149.

40 Lindsay Anderson, *About John Ford* (London: Plexus, 1981), p. 97.

41 Anderson, p. 9.

42 Andrew Sarris, *The John Ford Movie Mystery* (London: Secker & Warburg/BFI, 1976), p. 85.

43 Joseph McBride and Michael Wilmington, *John Ford* (London: Secker & Warburg, 1974), p. 53.

44 Ibid., p. 54.

45 Gallagher, p. 162.

46 See his entry in *The BFI Companion to the Western*.

47 *Hollywood Reporter*, 2 March 1939.

CREDITS
. . . .
Stagecoach

USA
Released 2 March 1939
British release
2 October 1939
Copyright date
20 February 1939
Distributed by
United Artists
Production company
Walter Wanger Productions
Inc.
Producer
Walter Wanger
Director
John Ford
Screenplay
Dudley Nichols
Original story
'Stage to Lordsburg'
by Ernest Haycox
Director of Photography
Bert Glennon
Art Director
Alexander Toluboff
Associate Art Director
Wiard B. Ihnen
Costumes
Walter Plunkett
Editorial Supervisor
Otho Lovering
Editor
Dorothy Spencer
Sound editor
Walter Reynolds
**Musical score based on
American folk songs
arranged by**
Richard Hageman, Franke
Harling, John Leipold, Leo
Shuken, Louis Gruenberg
Musical Direction
Boris Morros
Sound Engineer
Frank Maher
**Special Photographic
Effects**
Ray Binger

Assistant directors
Wingate Smith, Lowell
Farrell
Production Manager
Daniel Keefe
Assistant
Jack Kirston
Horsemen
Yakima Canutt, John Eckert,
Jack Mohr, Iron Eyes Cody
97 minutes
8,627 ft.

Claire Trevor
Dallas
John Wayne
The Ringo Kid
Andy Devine
Buck Rickabaugh
John Carradine
Hatfield
Thomas Mitchell
Dr Josiah Boone
Louise Platt
Lucy Mallory
George Bancroft
Sheriff Curly Wilcox
Donald Meek
Mr Samuel Peacock
Berton Churchill
Henry Gatewood
Tim Holt
Lt. Blanchard
Tom Tyler
Luke Plummer
Chris-Pin Martin
Chris
Cornelius Keefe
Captain Whitney
Francis Ford
Billy Pickett
Kent Odell
Billy Pickett Jr
Walter McGrail
Captain Sickels
Chief Big Tree
Indian Scout

Brenda Fowler
Mrs Gatewood
Lou Mason
Sheriff
Elvira Rios
Yakima, Chris's wife
Florence Lake
Mrs Nancy Whitney
Marga Ann Daighton
Mrs Pickett
Yakima Canutt
Cavalry scout
Harry Tenbrook
Telegrapher
Paul McVey
Express agent
Jack Pennick
Jerry the bartender
Joseph Rickson
Ike Plummer
Vester Pegg
Hank Plummer
William Hopper
Cavalry sergeant
Bryant Washburn
Captain Simmons
Nora Cecil
Dr Boone's landlady
Si Jenks
Merrill McCormick
Oglers
Jim Mason
Jim, an expressman
Helen Gibson
Dorothy Appleby
Dancing Girls
Buddy Roosevelt
Bill Cody
Cowboys
Chief White Horse
Geronimo
Ed Brady
Saloon keeper
Franklyn Farnum
Deputy
Mary Kathleen Walker
Lucy's baby

Duke Lee
Lordsburg sheriff
Theodore Lorch
Lordsburg express agent
Robert E. Homans
Editor in Lordsburg
Artie Ortega
Lordsburg barfly

With Steve Clemente, Fritzi Brunette, Leonard Trainor, Chris Phillips, Tex Driscoll, Pat Wayne, Teddy Billings, Al Lee, John Eckert, Jack Mohr, Patsy Doyle, Wiggie Blowne, Margaret Smith, Many Mules, Frank Baker, Navaho and Apache Indians.

The original negative of *Stagecoach* no longer exists. The print newly struck by the National Film Archive derives from duplicate mute and sound negatives acquired some time ago from Anthony Morris (London) Ltd., who used to represent the Walter Wanger library in the UK.

Stagecoach has been remade twice. The 1966 version, in CinemaScope and Technicolor, directed by Gordon Douglas, starred Ann-Margret as Dallas, Alex Cord as the Ringo Kid and Bing Crosby as Doc Boone. In 1986 Ted Post directed a Country and Western style remake, though without songs, with Willie Nelson in the Doc Boone role (now renamed as Doc Holliday), Kris Kristofferson as Ringo and Johnny Cash as Curly.

BIBLIOGRAPHY

1. Scripts

'Stagecoach', a film by John Ford and Dudley Nichols (London: Lorimer Publishing, 1971)

This script usefully reprints Ernest Haycox's original story 'Stage to Lordsburg'. Unfortunately, it is seriously inadequate as a transcription of what appears on the screen. For example, the script prints an opening legend: 'Until the Iron Horse came, the Stagecoach was the only means of travel on the untamed American frontier', etc. None of this is in Ford's film. Much of the dialogue is inaccurately rendered. At one point Buck justifies his decision to take the mountain route, up through the snow, on the grounds that the Apaches don't care for the cold. He refers to their scanty clothing – 'those breech-clout Apaches'. In the script as published this is rendered as 'those beach-crowd Apaches' – as if the Apache are some distant precursors of Californian surfers. Scarcely a page of this book is free of error. A reputable publishing house would surely withdraw this farrago and replace it with a proper scholarly text. Instead, Faber's 'revised' reprint of the script published in 1984 (no corrections are apparent) also contains an afterword by Andrew Sinclair, extracted from his book *John Ford: A Biography* (New York: Dial Press, 1979). This offers a touching account of how John Ford attended the funeral of Tom Mix in 1939, and how Ford was so moved that he vowed to recreate the old West as a testimony to his respect for Mix. Thus was *Stagecoach* born. It's a shame to spoil a good story, but Ford shot *Stagecoach* in the autumn of 1938. Tom Mix's fatal car crash did not occur until 12 October 1940.

Dudley Nichols' original script, differing in some significant respects from what Ford shot, was published in *Twenty Best Film Plays*, ed. John Gassner and Dudley Nichols (New York: Crown, 1943).

See also Richard Anobile, *Stagecoach* (New York: Avon, 1974), which presents the film shot by shot in frame stills with dialogue. Unfortunately the stills do not always show just what is on the screen, being presented in a variety of formats, only some of which correspond to the actual Academy ratio of the original.

2. Books about Ford

a. Biography
Ford, Dan. *Pappy: The Life of John Ford* (Englewood Cliffs, N.J.: Prentice-Hall, 1979). British title *The Unquiet Man: The Life of John Ford* (London: William Kimber, 1982).

Gallagher, Tag. *John Ford: The Man and his Films* (Berkeley: University of California Press, 1986).

Sinclair, Andrew. *John Ford: A Biography* (New York: Dial Press, 1979).

b. Commentary
Anderson, Lindsay. *About John Ford* (London: Plexus, 1981).

Baxter, John. *The Cinema of John Ford* (London: Zwemmer, 1971).

Bogdanovich, Peter. *John Ford* (London: Studio Vista, 1967).

Dayan, Daniel. *Western Graffiti* (Paris: Editions Clancier-Guenaud, 1983).

Leutrat, Jean-Louis and Liandrat-Guigues, Suzanne. *Les Cartes de l'Ouest* (Paris: Armand Colin, 1990).

McBride, Joseph, and Wilmington, Michael. *John Ford* (London: Secker & Warburg, 1974).

Mitry, Jean. *John Ford* (Paris: Editions Universitaires, 1954).

Place, J.A. *The Western Films of John Ford* (New York: Citadel, 1975).

Sarris, Andrew. *The John Ford Movie Mystery* (London: Secker & Warburg/BFI, 1976).

3. Articles

Behlmer, Rudy. 'Bret Harte in Monument Valley' in *America's Favorite Movies* (New York: Frederick Ungar, 1982).

Browne, Nick. 'The Spectator-in-the-Text: The Rhetoric of *Stagecoach*', *Film Quarterly*, Winter 1975.

Cahiers du Cinéma. No. 183, October 1966 (John Ford issue).

Leutrat, Jean-Louis and Liandrat-Guigues, Suzanne. 'Monument Valley dans l'oeuvre de John Ford: Une idée de réserve', *Vertigo*, nos. 6–7, 1991.

McCarthy, Todd. 'John Ford and Monument Valley', *American Film*, May 1978.

Positif. 'Dossier John Ford', nos. 353–4, July-August 1990.

Velvet Light Trap. No. 2, August 1971 (John Ford issue).

Thomas, Bob (ed.). 'John Ford and *Stagecoach*', *Action: Directors Guild of America* (September-October 1971).

Wide Angle. Vol. 2, no. 4, 1978 (John Ford issue).

BFI Film Classics '... could scarcely be improved upon ... informative, intelligent, jargon-free companions.'
The Observer

Each book in the BFI Publishing Film Classics series honours a great film from the history of world cinema. With new titles published each year, the series is rapidly building into a collection representing some of the best writing on film. If you would like to receive further information about future Film Classics or about other books from BFI Publishing, please fill in your name and address and return this card to the BFI.*

No stamp is needed if posted in the UK, Channel Islands, or Isle of Man.

NAME

ADDRESS

POSTCODE

*North America: Please return your card to:
Indiana University Press, Attn: LPB, 601 N Morton Street,
Bloomington, IN 47401-3797

BFI Publishing
21 Stephen Street
FREEPOST 7
LONDON
W1E 4AN